The Forest of Childhood

Poems from Sweden

EDITED AND TRANSLATED BY

WILLIAM JAY SMITH

LEIF SJÖBERG

New Rivers Abroad Book

New Rivers Press 1996

Copyright © 1996 by New Rivers Press
Library of Congress Catalog Card Number 91-61260
ISBN 0-89823-135-3
All Rights Reserved
Edited by Leif Sjöberg and William Jay Smith
Editorial Assistance by Paul J. Hintz
Cover photograph courtesy of the estate of George B. McCreary
Cover design by Gretchen Olson and Judy Gilats
Rosemaling by Gretchen Olson
Interior book design and typesetting by Peregrine Graphics Services

New Rivers Press is a non-profit literary press dedicated to publishing
the very best emerging writers in our region, nation, and world.

The publication of *The Forest of Childhood* has been made possible by
generous grants from the Elmer Anderson Foundation, the Beim Foun-
dation, the Bush Foundation, the General Mills Foundation, Liberty
State Bank, the McKnight Foundation, the Minnesota State Arts Board
(through an appropriation by the Minnesota Legislature), the Beverly J.
and John A. Rollwagen Fund of The Minneapolis Foundation, the Star
Tribune/Cowles Media Company, the Tankenoff Foundation, the Ten-
nant Company Foundation, the Wheatland Foundation and the con-
tributing members of New Rivers Press. New Rivers is a member
agency of United Arts.

The Forest of Childhood has been manufactured in Canada for New Rivers
Press, 420 North 5th Street, Minneapolis, MN 55401. First Edition.

*To the memory of
Muriel Rukeyser and
May Swenson whose
translations from the
Swedish have enriched
American poetry.*

Acknowledgments

Certain of these translations have appeared in the following books: *Agadir* by Artur Lundkvist, translated and with a preface by William Jay Smith and Leif Sjöberg (International Poetry Forum—Byblos Editions II, Pittsburgh, Pennsylvania), 1979: and *Wild Bouquet: Nature Poems* by Harry Martinson, translated, and with an introduction, by William Jay Smith and Leif Sjöberg (BkMk Press, Kansas City, Missouri), 1985. Others have appeared in the following journals, magazines, newspapers, and anthologies: *Anthology of Magazine Verse and Yearbook of American Poetry*, 1987, *The American Poetry Review, Books Abroad, The Christian Science Monitor, The International Portland Review, Mosaic* (Canada), *New Letters, The Painted Bride, Poetry East, The Scandinavian Review, The Structurist* (Canada), *Swedish Book Review, Swedish News*. The translators wish to thank these publications for permission to reprint.

The translation of "On the Outermost Edge" by Östen Sjöstrand appeared in the program for the inauguration of the Berwald Hall, Stockholm, 1979.

The translators wish to thank Tom Hedlund, from whose *Den Svenska Lyriken* (FIB, 1978) they have benefited for the headnotes in this volume.

Table of Contents

Introduction

Our selection of ten prominent Swedish poets of the twentieth century begins with the work of Johannes Edfelt, who was born in 1904 and who published his first book in 1923; it concludes with that of Elisabeth Rynell, born in 1954, who published her first book in 1975 and whose latest volume appeared in 1990. Thus it spans the greater part of the century and reflects some of the cataclysmic events that have shaped it. In his brilliant prose poem, "Drill at Nathanya," Johannes Edfelt, in a few lines, sums up the horror of the Holocaust. He writes incisively elsewhere of "the hairline edge between being and non-being," between "life's frenetic clamor and the eternity of absolute silence." Elisabeth Rynell's postmodernist sexual and psychological explorations, in a clipped and spare language suggestive of popular ballads, confront issues that are paramount in today's society. Far-ranging though it is, our survey of the century is by no means all-inclusive. The Finland-Swedish pioneers, Edith Södergran (1892–1925), Elmer Diktonius (1896–1961), and Gunnar Björling (1887–1960) are unfortunately not included although only Södergran is well represented in English. Also, the work of two preeminent poets, Gunnar Ekelöf (1907–1968) and Tomas Tranströmer (1931–   ), had to be omitted. Both are well known to the English-speaking world, Ekelöf in the powerful translations of Muriel Rukeyser and W. H. Auden, and Tranströmer in the equally forceful translations of May Swenson and Robert Bly. Although we have passed them over to make room for poets such as Lars Lundkvist, Kerstin Thorék, and Elisabeth Rynell, who are virtually unknown in English, their presence and influence are evident throughout.

Ekelöf was clearly the most original Swedish poet of the century. The poet's chief purpose, he thought, was to probe the unconscious, "to become like himself," and by doing so in mystical and dream poems, he helped introduce surrealism to Sweden. The surrealist technique is echoed in Artur Lundkvist's description of the effect of the earthquake in *Agadir*, in which Lundkvist turns with uncommon brilliance to the development of the individual image, which he calls "the most natural flower of the imagination, a center of delight." Ekelöf's mystical presence is felt in the contemplative and complex religious poetry of Östen Sjöstrand and in the magical folk evocations of Lars Lundkvist. Among the younger poets we present, the influence of Tranströmer is everywhere apparent. As Kerstin Thorék puts it, "Tranströmer's poetry constantly opens closed doors."

In Swedish poetry from the seventeenth century on, past Strindberg's "Indian Summer" and "Sunset by the Sea" down to the present, nature has been a favorite subject. All these poets may be seen as born allies of the botanist Carolus Linnaeus (1707–1778). Folke Isaksson's *Vinterresa* (*Winter Tour*, 1951), which beautifully reflects the landscape of northern Sweden, contains a moving portrait of Linnaeus. Harry Martinson is similar to the famous botanist, Lars Gyllensten points out, in his "deeply original ingenuity, his sensitive and unconventional alertness and attentiveness and also his humorous, unsentimental, and tender identification with the shape and form of every living thing." In Martinson's novel *The*

Road the core of central intelligence that shapes the wanderer's life is nature itself. His love of nature, which he details with microscopic precision, is intensified by his fear of losing it. In his epic poem *Aniara* (1956) the last spaceship from earth is on its way to Mars after the earth has been over-exploited and irradiated to the point that it can no longer sustain life. We have chosen *The Forest of Childhood* as the title of our collection because the poem by Harry Martinson presents an all-encompassing symbol of the nature celebrated throughout the book:

> Barefoot from tussock to tussock I ran
> seeking the farmer's cows,
> and saw how the mirrored firmament turned
> in the tarn its cloud-tufted wheel.
>
> In the summer's forests life played,
> and evening was deep with thrushes and the heaven high
>   with swallows.
> Nothing came of all my dreams and deceits,
> but memory enlivens my life
> and memories are completed dreams.
>
> To lingonberry patches deep in
> summer's own parish
> my dream migrates at times
> like a crane in spring.

Elisabeth Rynell, who went in 1977 to live in a village of ten inhabitants a thousand kilometers north of Stockholm, has called her encounters with the vast forests and the deer-herding Lapps "a kind of university." All these poets are in one way or another affected by the natural scene. Östen Sjöstrand finds in the dandelion a symbol of God's creation that outweighs all man's inventions. Even Lars Gustafsson, the most philosophical of the lot, addresses a moving ballad to the old paths in the province of Västmanland, where at the age of fourteen he had felt called upon to serve poetry with language "which in some mysterious way was identical with the wordless authority of the scenery."

The founder of Swedish poetry, Georg Stiernhielm (1598–1672), traveled widely in his youth and was inspired by what he saw. The Swedish poets of this century have also been great travelers, as the poems collected here indicate, and Swedish poetry has been open as never before to foreign influence. It was perhaps his many early years at sea that gave Harry Martinson the eye of such a careful, accurate, and objective observer. Artur Lundkvist, who traveled to all parts of the world, is as effective in evoking the landscape of Louisiana as he is the devastation of a catastrophic earthquake in Morocco.

Östen Sjöstrand gives us "Hamlet in Dubrovnik;" Folke Isaksson summons up an Appalachian spring; and Lars Gustafsson takes us to Mexico:

> In such rarefied air could a swallow
> find a place to rest its wing?

Kerstin Thorék, in her *Quipous* suite, evokes the Andes, "that rise higher than the castle of the condors." Travel, of course, can be directed inward as well as outward. Harry Martinson, the former sailor, used the trade wind as a symbol linking the extroverted traveler, the "world nomad," and the brooding introvert. Dream, including nightmare, plays an important role in Johannes Edfelt's prose poems. In one dream he goes speechless, numb, to his mother's deathbed, mindful that she gave him life. In another he hears a "metaphysical" scream: "it is a heaven-storming cry of absence . . . it is a cry for the God who does not exist." Lars Gustafsson writes of the balloonists, in a poem of that name, who climb ever upward through "air that is thinner than that of winter . . . until the very memory of them sings faintly like glass." In the title poem of Gustafsson's *A Trip to the Center of the Earth* (1966), he speaks of traveling to earth's core as envisioned in a dream. Lars Lundkvist, in his gnomic poems, has a cutting way of revealing the psychological states of ordinary people:

> She put on a green skirt
> and flew away in a cloud across southern Sweden.
>
> Her intention was unclear.
> Was she looking for her lover,
>
> a pastry-cook or a county police commissioner,
> the county council's director of invalids
>
> or a grocer?
> Her purpose was unclear.

Kerstin Thorék, haunted by Caravaggio, who painted "revolting physiognomies" and in whose work "even pimps are canonized," has the painter speak out in "The Medusa":

> I painted myself as that fury in the convex
> rounded shield. My severed head with the dark halo
> of writhing bronze serpents, I stare at you across the
>   centuries.

The effect of such psychic probing, evident throughout these pages, can indeed be riveting.

These poet-travelers have been amazingly successful in bringing back from their travels the poetry of other countries. As the headnotes in this volume reveal, they have all, particularly Johannes Edfelt and Artur Lundkvist, introduced and translated poets of almost every major language, and a number of minor ones, and have thus educated and enriched themselves, one another, and the Swedish public. The translation of Swedish poetry in this country, which has been spearheaded by Leif Sjöberg, is but a small repayment of the debt we owe these poets for their untiring efforts to make American poetry better known in Sweden.

I first became acquainted with Swedish poetry twenty years ago when, late in his life, W. H. Auden decided that he could no longer continue the translation of modern Swedish poets, particularly Harry Martinson and Artur Lundkvist, which he had undertaken with Leif Sjöberg, and suggested that I replace him. I felt honored to do so, and in the years since I have held Auden's strong, straightforward but graceful renderings as models to emulate. Auden's version of Martinson's "The Cable Ship" reads as if it had flowed directly his own pen:

> On latitude 15 degrees North, longitude 61 degrees West,
> between Barbados and Tortuga, we fished up the Atlantic
>   cable,
> held up our lanterns
> and pasted fresh rubber over the wound in its back.
> When we put our ears to the injured spot,
> we heard how it hummed inside.
>
> One of us said:
> "It is the millionaires in Montreal and Saint Johns who are
>   speaking
> about the price of sugar from Cuba and the lowering of
>   our wages."
>
> In a circle of lanterns we stood there long and thought,
> we patient cable fishermen,
> then we lowered the mended cable
> down to its home in the sea.

I feel privileged to have been introduced to a poetry so rich and diverse, and laboring to bring it over into English has been its own reward. Now in the work of these ten poets, ranging from Kjell Hjern's playful but cutting ironic observations to Östen Sjöstrand's profound and somber meditations on modern technology, I hope the reader will find more than a modicum of that rich diversity.

—*William Jay Smith*

xvi

Johannes Edfelt
(1904–   )

Johannes Edfelt, poet, translator, and essayist, has enjoyed a long and distinguished literary career. Since 1968 he has been a member of the Swedish Academy and served on its Nobel Committee from 1974 to 1989. The bibliography of his published works comprises more than 250 pages. His poems from six decades *Ekolodning* (Echo Sounding, hard cover edition, 1986) ran to twelve thousand copies. In the United States a comparable edition would be 350,000 copies.

Edfelt has done marvelous yeoman service as a translator from several languages. He began with his lyrical versions of German, English, and American poetry in 1940. He has produced twenty-two volumes of translations in all, and, in 1989, Bonniers published *Följeslagare* (Companions), an anthology comprising his versions of poems by no less than thirty-nine German-language poets, thirteen French-language poets, nineteen British and Irish poets, and ten Americans. Names such as Goethe, Hölderlin, Rilke, Hesse, Trakl, Kafka, Benn, Baudelaire, Verlaine, Apollinaire, Yeats, Eliot, Spender, Whitman, Frost, Walcott, and Pound speak for themselves.

Edfelt was born in Kyrkefalla in the province of Västergötland, in south-central Sweden. He says that as far back as he can trace them, to the beginning of the eighteenth century, most of his forebears on both sides of the family have lived in Västergötland

and made their living as freeholders in exchange for providing equestrian knights to the crown, or as owner-farmers. One of them belonged to the Västgöta Cavalry and died in the Swedish-German War in 1759. In some of his poems —"Vestrogothica," for instance —he apostrophizes his ancestors, their workplaces and ultimate resting places.

While still a teenager, Edfelt made his debut in 1923 with a book of melancholy verse he later disavowed, as he did his next three collections: none of them appear in his collected poems.

Edfelt keeps his distance and is certainly not a confessional poet, but one of his student-friends at the University of Uppsala, Wilhelm Fischer, has revealed in a memoir what appears to be an important confession of sorts. The time referred to is the late twenties, when Freud's theories had begun to gain some currency even in Sweden, and liberation could easily have been a topic for discussion. Interestingly, Edfelt told his friend how he had once caught his father at a desperate juncture and wrested a pistol out of his hand. That very act set Johannes Edfelt free and, no doubt, gave him a self-confidence he had previously lacked.

We know that Edfelt's father was a soldier: is it unreasonable to assume there was more than a fair amount of discipline in the young man's home, that freedom was hard to come by, and the lack of it might have affected the young man's outlook on life? In any case, it is possible to recognize in Edfelt's "forbidden music" in *Högmässa* (High Mass, 1934) the temptation suicide exerted on the persona of one or two of his poems.

The prose poem is a genre in which the French and the Americans excel. But Edfelt manages to hold his own, as W. H. Auden himself acknowledged by translating some of them. Although Edfelt occasionally oscillates between his perception of the world as it is and his dream-perception of how the world ought to be, there is a remarkable consistency in his lyrical style. He is like a painter, searching for a relatively stable light before he begins to fill his canvases.

In "The Eye of the Cyclone" he asks himself, "what do you yourself, ambulating figure, rootless poet, put up against Nothing?" He gives several answers: the white shimmer over the birch trees on a January day, and other matters pertaining to light (which to him is precious and sublime), but above all he tries to maintain his effort "to keep alive his dream of freedom in beauty, an inner freedom."

It is moving to note that as a septuagenarian (in *Brev* [Letter], 1976), Edfelt addressed a hidden well-spring—but not one guarded by an Arethusa—thus: "the way to you was the way to my innermost being." Assuming that he is referring to the function of poetry in the creator himself, the statement is an endorsement of creativity as sanity and freedom. The creative spirit, not relationships with gods and people, has brought about whatever unity there has been in this poet's life: that appears to be why, in spite of life's difficulties, he is eager and courageous enough to serve poetry to the end. Poetry gives essential meaning to his life.

Closing Down the Railroad

The rails and sleepers of the narrow gauge railroad are long gone. The embankment will soon be overgrown with common plantain, dandelion, bindweed, and pigweed: and anything more redundant than the abandoned station house and the railway signal, that one-armed spectre, is hard to imagine. The last handcar stands in a shed on its three wheels collecting a layer of dust; the station master's whistle is rusting in a corner, and if you could hear the weeds grow, you could also hear the moth gorge itself on the once flamboyant signal flag, now in a closet and unused for many years.

Two

To Brita Elisabet Ester

Your hand in mine, together we go toward evening and ashes. You, whose steps I hear at my side, the wounds of your life became mine, your sorrow and your joy echoed within me like fugues in organ-pipes. Your hand in mine—until, when the time comes, one of us will loosen his grip on the other and glide down into the namelessness of night.

George Gissing: In Memoriam

To others the victory wreath, to you the memorial tribute of a few survivors. You saw London as a sick organ; in your diagnosis, it became a gigantic, electrically vibrating conglomerate of misery, vice, epidemics, neuroses, and distorted, hopeless ambitions. You saw the multitudes of the slum, as gray as lemmings. You knew the brutality of the law that governed: "Money or your life." You labored yourself in the shiny, thread-bare lines of literature's proletarians. After a day of grueling work, you would duck into some cheap eating place and then quickly disappear into your lonely hovel. There you fixed onto paper the detailed visions of a world to which science, under the thin surface of civilization, has brought back a barbarism more inexorable than that of the savage. So— at the end of a life of toil, the liberated breathing of Henry Ryecroft. And then death's cruel, swift hand that puts a stop to everything.

Drill at Nathanya

As strange as it would be to encounter a five-legged zebra on the street was it to see in the park at Nathanya, the new city on the coast of Israel, that man in his elegant khaki-colored suit with the camera on his chest, halting at every tenth step that he took, clicking his heels and bellowing some commands in German, while his right arm, like a semaphore, struck out in a salute, fatally reminiscent of the one that at one time was prescribed in the country that thought itself solidly established for a thousand years. One, two, three . . . ten steps, then, click—he stood at attention and roared out a corporal's commands. It was not long before with your inner eye you saw him with his exterior completely transformed: it was no longer in a khaki-colored suit that he drilled but in the striped rags of the concentration camp; and behind the unfortunate figure rose the smoke from the chimneys of the gas ovens, thick and black against the ash-gray heavens.

Network of Roads

The old village roads are the landscape's fine sinuous net of arteries. How softly these gravel arteries meander forth over the terrain, avoiding hills and outcroppings of stone. Under summer skies they are lined with luminous strings of lady's bedstraw and dandelions. The wanderer on these deserted roads often encounters a milestone, where beneath a thin crust of lichen is outlined the Carolingian monogram cxi. Carts and surreys, hay wagons and open-sided wagons, have for centuries followed these sinuous lines. The day laborer in the summer heat and the autumn rains has here shouted at his oxen; bridal couples have journeyed toward their new home; death's black chariot has slowly rolled forth toward that resting place, where all our roads will some day end.

The Signal

He awaits a signal of a sort that he thinks cannot be compared to any he has heard over the years. Its quality cannot be that of the bugle blast from an autumnal birch grove nor that of the roll of drums, exhorting soldiers to break camp, nor that of the bass drum when a parade begins to move out. He knows not whether it is as strong as the noise of a waterfall or as weak as the whine of a wood mouse. He knows only that it is a signal that during the fraction of a second is poised on the hair-line edge between being and nonbeing.

Largo

Reverence and fear fill us when we are confronted with the darkly incorruptible truth of life's most extreme and final movements: the hare's last steep dismayed tumble, when it received the deadly shot from the bold green-clad hunter; the stock dove's incredible curve, before its downy body, hit by buckshot, reaches the ground—the warm spool's final journey in September-clear air is forever inscribed on one's retina. The irrevocable provokes shudders, the irreversible rivets us. But who will deny that the final and most extreme also has a sublimity beyond all else: death has sculpted it. Even the suicide's painful image shares it. Suddenly you wish to hide your face before the incredible loneliness of the movement of his hand, the most extreme, final movement when he brings the ampoule of poison to his mouth or the revolver to his temple and in one split second hangs on the knife-edge between life's frenetic clamor and the eternity of absolute silence.

Harry Martinson
(1904–1978)

Poets lead notoriously difficult lives, but surely few poets anywhere have begun life under more trying circumstances than Harry Martinson. When his alcoholic, sea-faring father died in 1910, his mother fled to California, leaving the six-year-old Harry, along with her four other youngest children, to public welfare. After humiliating years with his guardians, he ran away to sea at the age of fourteen, and from 1920 to 1927 shipped out fourteen times, serving under the flags of various nations, in his words, "as deck-hand, stoker, coaltrimmer, and all-round kitchen menace on eighteen ships, sometimes bumming around in the ports of the world, hiking for thousands of miles, especially in India, on the European continent, and in the Americas." Having acquired tuberculosis at sea, he came ashore for good, and his disease was arrested. Like Melville, whom he resembles in many ways, he spent the remainder of his life making use of these early experiences in his work. His first travel books, collected in English in the volume *Cape Farewell* (1934), won him wide acclaim, as did his fictionalized autobiography *Flowering Nettle* (1935, English translation, 1936.) In *Passad* (Trade Winds, 1945) he abandoned traveling in an outward sense; instead he traveled inwardly, seeking the ties between the extrovert traveler, the "world nomad," and the brooding introvert. The former sailor employed the concept of "trade wind" as a unifying symbol. "There exists something universally compelling that cannot yet be pinned down in a material way," he wrote. "The wind is a good symbol of this, and among the winds the trade wind is the best symbol of human reasonableness and of the human desire for airing things. It symbolizes a mental state that takes the sea atmosphere as a model, its openness uniting with the eye's openness for new vistas and new lands." The metaphor of travel acquired a new dimension in Martinson's epic poem *Aniara* (1956, adapted from the Swedish by Elspeth Harley Schubert and Hugh MacDiarmid, introduction by Tord Hall, New York, Knopf, 1963; a new English translation by Stephen Klass and Leif Sjöberg, will be published by Story Line Press.) The poem tells of a giant spaceship hurtling through the universe on an irreversible journey with 8,000 evacuees on board, after technological man has made the earth uninhabitable and all imaginative possibilities have been neglected or rejected. After the publication of *Aniara*, most critics hailed Martinson as a "pioneer of the poetry of the Atomic Age." In 1949 Martinson was elected to the Swedish Academy and in 1974 he shared the Nobel Prize for literature with Eyvind Johnson.

Aniara continues to be interpreted very differently. Wittgenstein's successor at Cambridge University, Georg von Wright, reads the poem as a requiem for a civilization approaching a global environmental catastrophe, while the Martinson expert, Ingvar Holm, suggests it is an optimistic work, basically appealing to modern man not to go From One World to None, as the Aniarians do, but to save the world ecologically by insights and sensible actions.

Martinson's novel *The Road* (1948, English translation, 1955) preceded Jack Kerouac's *On the Road*, and although it shares perhaps the latter book's impetus of protest against the evils of organized society, it is wholly different. The guiding spirit of Martinson's novel is a central intelligence, a focus of feeling that gives form to the wanderer's life. At the core of this intelligence is nature itself: "There were a thousand reasons why one walked the highways year after year. One of the loveliest of those reasons was the woods, the forest. The woods had a way of hiding themselves behind themselves from tree to tree, from ridge to ridge, and of never ceasing to give promise of something hidden. Associated with the woods was a great and hopeless attraction. There was no banishing it, for if you tried to drive it away, it merely flitted like a bird from tree to tree, called like a cuckoo or whistled like a thrush. . . . If you went into the forest as a child, idly, or just to pick berries or to look for strayed cows, then the whole forest stepped forward, closed round you, poured its waves over you, and you were caught, at once terrified and expectant. The forest by its constant change of shape and sound persuaded the wanderer who walked in it that he must ever expect something, darkly urging upon him foreboding after foreboding, presentiment after presentiment, without end."

Early in his career Martinson abandoned private symbolism and experience in his poetry for the largest theme of all, nature. He allied himself with a fine Swedish tradition that began even before the time of Linnaeus (1707–1778). From a few square feet of the natural scene that the poet studies and observes, he finds his way to a broad, and even cosmic, perspective and to a magnanimous philosophy of life. Martinson's years at sea gave him a sense of distance that makes him at all times a careful and accurate observer. As in the paintings of Degas, the distancing power of the artist's sharp eye makes for a remarkable kind of ironic tension. His subjects seem at the same time intimately warm and yet incongruously cold, as if fixed far-off in time and space. He looks on the peonies in bloom in his summer garden in the same timeless way as on the drifting Florida seaweed in this poem, translated by W. H. Auden:

Out At Sea

Out at sea one feels a spring or a summer merely as a
passing breeze.
Sometimes in the summer the drifting Florida seaweed
blooms,
and on a spring evening a spoon-bill stork flies in towards
Holland.

If the tone of voice in "Out at Sea" rings true, it is perhaps, as
Auden suggested, because the poet establishes the sea as the cen-
ter on which traffic moves in time and space, as through the sailor's
consciousness, in real dimensions and in the reader's mind.

The poems included here are from *Wild Bouquet: Nature
Poems*, translated, and with an introduction, by William Jay Smith
and Leif Sjöberg, Book Mark Press, University of Missouri, Kansas
City, 1985. First drafts of several of the translations were done by
W. H. Auden, to whose memory *Wild Bouquet* is dedicated; the
version of "The Song of the Thrush" is almost entirely his.

The Moment

Before the moment bursts and perishes,
the dragon-fly sits by the water-mirror.
Each second a striking of death's clock,
each minute a funeral cortege of seconds.
Let us linger closely by the moment
now that the moth grazes against eternity
before the moment bursts and perishes.

Giant Spruce

The giant spruce; almost a forest in itself
with its own storm song.
Like everything in its own life but also all of life.
Alone in the noise of multitudes,
itself a quantity of secret places and fates.
Silent winters, haystackcloud summers,
pigeon and marten.
At its top often a thrush
singing of the years,
long and many,
that go sweeping by.

Winter Piece

Delicate ermine tracks
cross lightly
in eights on the winter snow
there where a hidden ice-brook with its white fur roof
winds forward,
there where the swirling water had scooped out
a rippling bowl,
the otter drinks from the ice-eye.
When the children in red woolen caps come
to hear the singing of this polar roof,
the otter digs into his cave
and watches their eyes through chinks in the ice.

Dwarf Juniper

Nothing can more harshly interpret
life's enduring struggle
than a dwarf juniper on a coastal heath.
Dumbfounded, you read
its hard-life text,
its created contortion,
with its fierce-creeping battle-grip,
swept into stiffened spirals by gale winds.

Tussock

The tussock soaks up the sun
and quietly and slowly expels
the frost from its earth-body.
It spurs on its growth with spring sighs of accumulated warmth.
The tongues and edges of the nearest snowdrifts
shrink visibly in the spring gale.
The drippings from the roof begin to mark time in the barrel.

Cuckoo

The voice of spring is heard in the forest.
Everyone named Otto
believes that the cuckoo is calling him.
But the cuckoo is merely auctioning off
his bankrupt estate.
Soon he will board out his son.

The Forest of Childhood

Barefoot from tussock to tussock I ran
seeking the farmer's cows,
and saw how the mirrored firmament turned
in the tarn its cloud-tufted wheel.

In the summer's forests life played,
and evening was deep with thrushes and the heaven high
     with swallows.
Nothing came of all my dreams and deceits,
but memory enlivens my life
and memories are completed dreams.

To lingonberry patches deep in
summer's own parish
my dream migrates at times
like a crane in spring.

The Song of the Thrush

Somewhere in the forest evening sits a thrush. We cannot see him, but his song spreads abroad wider and wider like the ripples on a pond. Though it brings relief and is entirely unoppressive, what we mean by sadness and by "far-away" is there, everywhere among the silent motionless spruce trees—and the evening sun paints the tall trunks of the pine trees with that very color: far away.

Everywhere on earth, but above all in its forests, resound such remote and expressive strings and what is meant by divination rushes restlessly over heaths and valleys. Lights and shadows of the same timbre come and go, liberate and bind. The ear begins to search. Where is the thrush sitting? Perhaps here, perhaps there. The eye helps the ear choose trees, but the song spirals down from so many hundreds of branches that it fades away and makes a riddle of itself. And new tones come, or are they forever the same? Now are heard the tones of an inhaled melody. They seem to be moving backwards, thrown against the distant background. It seems to the ear as if a whole cubic mile on either side of the thrush is filled with this piercingly gentle inhalation.

Instinctively he perches where the entrance to the forest valley becomes like a giant Tibetan lure, instinctively perches on the right branch, located where the air is like an eardrum.

Somewhere in this very forest, in the still of the evening, among its thousand peaks, echo has its most sensitive crossroads. One can hear him trying out many different places and trees until he finds the very one which at this particular moment has the greatest resonance.

He wishes to be heard and to hear himself spread his evening speech more richly and purely than ever before. But first his instrument has to be tuned. This he does by flying around to discover where, in the spaces of the forest, the most sensitive chords are heard this particular evening.

It may take him an hour or two before he manages to find out how the layers of air tonight stand tuned in relation to each other.

"Yes! Here!" he sometimes seems to cry. And then he tries out the atmospheric possibilities of that spot. But there is a heaviness in the air that he must tune away. More accurately than any mathematician he soon discovers that the worst part was caused by a current of air, rising from some small remote dell in the recesses of the forest. His song must be repeated. But where? In some places he utters only a few notes. They are enough to tell him that this is not the right place. He flies off again.

Sometimes he comes near to despair. Will he never perhaps find the right music? Will he never find the tall pine tree where the finest inhaled tones of the bird flute are in accordance with the whims and laws of the air-realm?

Well, at long last, he comes near to it. Perfect he cannot be. Once in a thousand years perhaps, by sheer chance a single thrush achieves perfection. But he comes near to it, perches in the vicintiy of clarity. The layers of air are fairly well outwitted, the echo possibilities fairly well employed in the direction he wishes.

Then he strikes up his song, a small thrush playing on a giant instrument, enormous masses of relatively obedient air cleanly absorbing and cleanly reproducing the sounds of his throat-flute.

Thus he sings for a long time until dusk falls, and his song now conveys the image of the curve of a remote bow, strung together in the world of longing, with its honesties and dishonesties on a thread of the question that vanishes in the direction of the great Clock of Nothingness as it dissolves within the core of the setting sun.

Butterflies

Butterflies have no wings.
They fly by means of voluminous oriental shawls.
In this way nature has helped them.
She has created these beautiful shawls
so that the butterfly shall be harder to swallow.

Swan

Voraciously the swan
with the white crook of its neck,
a slanting sickle,
cuts into the forest of chickweed,
bores with the awl of its beak
into the putrid velvet of sludge,
raises its head and looks
coldly as a snake about the bay of dreams.

Sphinx-Moth and Daddy Longlegs

In the evening when dark is settling down, the stately sphinx-moth comes to the wild honeysuckle by the rock face. At dusk when one's impressions of color are blurred, it somewhat resembles a hummingbird in front of the flowers in a Brazilian forest glade. It has the same admirable ability with flickering intensity to stand still in the air, at which point the fantastic frequency of oscillation can no longer be perceived except as a cloud-image of whirling powder in the soft gray-white light. On its long trunk is a straw that appears to support and control the hovering level.

It is like a flying, peaceful honey-stiletto, whose wings function with dizzying precision. When its long honey-stick has sucked up the secreted supply in the deep, narrow hiding places of the flower, it recoils an inch or more and then moves sideways to the next flower.

For five or six evenings in a row it searches throughout the entire honeysuckle growth that covers almost half the rock face.

The sphinx-moth is among the twilight's *noctuidae* moths, those that have the firmest and most inviting appearance. It has none of the daddy longlegs's spooky thinness and endless long-legged vacillation. The sphinx-moth always seems to have an errand, while the daddy longlegs seems always to be coming at random like a spindle-thin emaciated piece of wreckage, carried about by the wind. The placid, cautiously strutting daddy longlegs is thinner even than the harvester-beetle. But it exists, it feeds itself and manages as we do. When it is smashed by an impatient hand, it quietly collapses. Then its remains mark the wall like a Chinese ink-drawn character, its legs stretched out like a lingering fragment in the frozen billows of death.

And there outside the wall flies the sphinx-moth with its proud, lynx-marked body. And men, who are so far removed from insects, try to bring their thoughts into harmony with them, but they never can.

Mystery seeps through all the crevices, and the clocks tick on. Reality arches itself in the mind as in a crucible. Man, the seeker, seeks himself.

The Henhouse

The hens, arriving early from the day's pickings,
circle a few times around the henhouse floor
and arrange themselves in the current pecking order.
Only when this is made clear
do they leap up to the roost.
Soon they're all seated in rows around the rooster.
He makes a stab or two at sleeping
but there will be no sleep for a while.
The hens fuss and shove.
With peck and cawkle, he must quiet them down.
Then there is a shifting and settling:
one of the hens tries to remember the latest
worm she caught,
but the memory is already fading,
on its way down her crop.
Another hen, on the edge of sleep, recalling clearly
the rooster's prowess, rolls her eyes heavenward,
her fluttering eyelids shutting out the world.

Peonies

Summer grew, broadened out;
thickened into positive clumps.
Dark-red farm peonies bulged in the rain.
When they opened their firm-knotted rag balls, she came by,
the lusty queen.
She looked for heavy bouquets,
luxuriant repasts for the senses.
The greenery was wet. Life-wet was the summer-saga:
She had prepared only for life, not for autumn.
Deep in her flesh defiantly she knew
that in time Death would wave to her
with his banner of hay.

Wild Bouquet

Gathered into a bouquet, the restless bluebells tremble,
try to break through your absent-minded, wide-eyed gaze,
with summer still here, dry and seedy.
Radiant long dry days with a desiccating solar wind;
from fragile, hairlike grass falls a dandruff of seeds.
Wake up, my great-eyed dreaming girl,
get back here before autumn takes over!

The Final Year

It was the year when the abandoned cottage in the woods
    was sold for firewood.
The woodcutters came with their truck
and tore it down in three hours and a quarter
and even took with them the well-frame.
It was so small when they detached it from the well
that they did not bother to smash it
but put it up on the bed of the truck just as it was.
And there it sat, a little gray chest covered with moss.

When all was quiet again
the weasel came out of the old fireplace.
It summoned a cuckoo from the woods,
and the two of them held a devotional hour.
The cuckoo sang a cuckoo hymn.
By then everything was over:
Nothing after that was as it was before.
But still the summer sauntered forth,
loosening its grasses and garlands.

Cutting Firewood in Autumn

When we cut firewood in the late autumn forest
many things happened that the senses preserved,
things that lay down in memory, fueling it with their
    own shiny birch bark.
That part of the firewood never went up in smoke.
The wedge needed
to split gnarled wood
was beaten into memory as well.
When the halved logs were split and stacked,
all the years of the birch burst open,
six feet at a time,
with the smell of summer and winter.
The memory of weariness was driven away
as the woodpile grew higher.
Memory guards the fine white bureau of cord wood
in the middle of the autumn forest.

Santa Claus

Each year when the trees turn white
the hateful old smiler returns,
the nursery's Rasputin. He shakes his cotton-wad beard
and high-booted forces his way into everybody's heart.

Tropical Myth

Rain cast its net over the forest,
caught drought's demon.
Lightning held high its lantern,
flickered, went out, was lit again
until it was all over and the trees shook off the moisture.
Everything became clear again.
The apes wove
the ascending moon
into a loose-braided basket of lianas.
The moon escaped
but dropped embers
on the buzzarding caraya monkeys in the branches
of the mora trees:
That is how fireflies were born.

Nature Sculpture in the Andes

The seething random rain, the scraping ice
have from this granite sculptured a maiden.

Lichen clings with its green wool
to the patchy rock face
around the rock-navel's mound,
around the loins of gneiss.
In vain ants tickle
the stone maiden's enormous granite teats.
Lightning has struck her neck.
She's been leaning here for a thousand years
and scoffs at lightning and all
with a grooved ice-grin. Three-armed. One-eyed.
An eternal gaze goes forth from her side eye
of quartz. By her calf the brook
speaks of dethroned just gods,
sings with wet silver bells
by the smooth giant ankle.

Sorrow and Joy

Every deep sorrow has lost joy as its object.
Do not lose that direction.
Do not let sorrow forget its errand.
Sorrow is the deepest honor that joy can obtain.

The Departure of Memories

When memories are about to depart they come more often
as if they wished to be wholly consumed.
It is best to consume them like a favorite dish
so often that they are no longer desired.
Their value is thus diminished
so that one day they fall prey to bold oblivion.

Artur Lundkvist
(1906–1991)

Artur Lundkvist was a short-story writer, novelist, essayist, and translator, but above all a poet. In 1927 he translated poems by Edgar Lee Masters and Carl Sandburg, and the following year made his debut with *Glöd* (Fervor, or Embers, 1928, new edition, 1966), a collection of free verse, influenced by Elmer Diktonius, Sandburg, Walt Whitman, and the early Pär Lagerkvist. These poems express ecstatic attitudes toward life and boundless faith in human instincts and drives. With this book, Lundkvist became the strongest force in Swedish modernist poetry. It was followed by some eighty books of poetry, fiction, and essays. Throughout his career as a writer and member of the Swedish Academy, Lundkvist tirelessly continued, with his translations, to introduce contemporary authors, often Americans, to Swedish readers.

Several of Artur Lundkvist's books contain poems relating to his many journeys to different parts of the world as well as portrait poems of writers or artists whom he knew or admired, like "The South: Louisiana," "Melville, America," and "Van Gogh" included here. One of his most memorable long poems, which we excerpt, concerns an earthquake that struck the port and resort city of Agadir on the coast of Morocco on March 1, 1960, killing almost all of its inhabitants. Artur Lundkvist and his wife, poet Maria Wine, were among the survivors. In *Agadir* (translated and with a Preface by William Jay Smith and Leif Sjöberg, International Poetry Forum, Byblos Editions II, 1979), written on his return to Sweden after days of brooding on the experience, lyrical reportage is raised to its highest level, and the result is a literary document of enduring importance.

A poet chooses his or her subject, but the subject also chooses the poet, who must be ready for it when it comes. In this instance, Artur Lundkvist, for whom the visual imagination had always been supremely important, was prepared. An early student of surrealism, although never narrowly limited by it, Lundkvist says of poetry that it "constitutes a constantly undecided struggle between reality and dream, reality and imagination, day and night, individual and humanity, man and cosmos." In this struggle, brilliantly recorded in *Agadir*, the most important means of expression is the image or compilation of images. The image—for Lundkvist "the most natural flower of the imagination, a center of delight"—establishes "the lightning-quick relationships of the imagination between phenomena of different types . . . the real task of poetry."

Lundkvist's exploration of the catastrophe is not philosophical like that of Voltaire in his *Poème sur le dèsastre de Lisbonne* (1756). Voltaire, examining in the aftermath of the Lisbon quake the question of evil in nature, attacks the doctrine of a benevolent Providence. Nor is Lundkvist passionate like Kleist in "The Earthquake in Chile," with its metaphysical problems. Nor does Lundkvist in his reporting view the ruins with the scientific eye of the young Darwin aboard the *Beagle* when the ship sailed into Talcahuano Bay after an earthquake that uncovered layers of historic and prehistoric life. Lundkvist's point of reference is always human, and his vision of suffering humanity gives the poem its power. His presentation of the victims huddled together on the shore, a "human community, beyond languages and races, in speechless waiting," is unforgettable. The premonitory dove in the opening section, "made of light and snow" and appearing as if the messenger of some magic domain, is at the same time "high-bosomed like a singer." The poet makes clear that it is in human terms that the whole experience will unfold, and that its full tragic convolutions will not rule out segments of humor. Men and their machines are from the beginning contrasted with natural creatures: the helicopter appears at the same time as the locusts from the desert. Man's confidence in his "unshakable order over nature" is completely destroyed when disaster strikes. The poem reaches its climax when the narrator and his wife move among the rubble of man's artifacts, and when from the deathly quiet rise the human soliloquies: that of the husband whose blonde wife drowns in the warm bath she has taken to forget a film she has just seen, and of the fifteen-year-old Moslem bride "whose real life has lasted only one night." These dislocated voices rise from the ruins as from the deepest levels of the subconscious, and through them the narrator identifies with all humanity. (In a radio interview Artur Lundkvist revealed that his marriage was close to breaking up just prior to the Agadir earthquake (Anaïs Nin's diaries).

Agadir, the shining white city, becomes to the poet's inner eye a city in which life is clasped by death, a mirage forever reminding him of what may lie in store for humanity:

> the greater destruction,
> a world in ruins, earth laid waste, only Death
> trailing smoke and disappearing into space.

While delivering a lecture on Anthony Burgess in 1981, Artur Lundkvist suffered a massive heart attack, and lay in a coma for more than two months. "Despite the doctors' disparagements," Maxine Kumin writes, "Lundkvist's wife came to the hospital twice a day to sing to his inert form, read poems, and recount their shared experiences while he lay there, eyes open but unseeing, lungs breathing with the help of a respirator. After six weeks, amazingly, he began to rouse for brief periods. When his breathing tube was removed, he was instantly able to speak. His knowledge of five languages returned to him intact. And as he recovered from his ordeal, he began to record the strange and vivid journeys that he had taken during his long coma. In the resulting *Journeys in Dream and Imagination* (translated by Ann B. Weissmann and Annika Planck, introduction by Carlos Fuentes, New York, Four Walls Eight Windows, 1991), Lundkvist makes leaps that are truly breathtaking and startlingly apt. But more than anything, *Journeys in Dream and Imagination* is a tribute to human courage. As Carlos Fuentes suggests, Lundkvist "has never been beaten, he has simply been, all this time, at the center of an unfathomable mystery . . . at the epiphany where our awareness of humanity is our innermost self."

Melville, America

I

He had spent his youth at sea, had read
the ocean's books, leafed through islands' leaves, waded
through the whale's brain, felt the heat of love's cheek.
The sails breathed in his chest like albatross wings
while he lived shut up in a house amid stifling trees—
with a woman as tough as a beached boat
in a landlocked love without waves or depths.

His thoughts darkened before the red eye of the night lamp,
the morning's birds numbly touched their brass tongues.
The world's wailing he bore within himself, a bellowing
from oceans and sunken peaks. The horizon
revealed not a single sail. And in vain he sought
the traces of a man's feet, broad as the leaves of waterlilies.

Why did dust form on the lagoons of temptation?
Why did he see fires far off between tree trunks,
and the whale's giant fin against the sky when it dived
to suck giant squid from the caverns of the deep,
and a mad man with breakers around his forehead—
aboard a death-ship rattling with dry laurel?

O love deep-sunken like a white tombstone
or like a sail unfurling its unwritten poem!

II

Boots marked by the teeth of wild beasts,
teeth that had killed a stag beside the ruin,
river disappearing forever into the mountain and
skin goose-pimpled under the tattooer's gaze:
a man with his umbilical cord in the sea, in quest of
the stone of reality,
threatened by the whale-oil-barrel pulpit, and weighed down
by a petrified maternal bosom.

Oh, shipwrecked, to live on beloved comrades' flesh salted by
sea water,
and then to be punished by rescue on a deserted island with
pepper-grass and sickening eggs,
thrown out into his endless memory of oceans, lured by
merciless distances and hurricanes,
where man was doomed to hang fluttering from mast or
tentpole, worn to a rag by the wind,
more and more enslaved by victories over nature!

Outside of time, cleft between dark and light, with the
salt-throb of the ocean in his blood,
he was the ocean rider, helpless on land like the albatross,
his wings uselessly trailing,
a harpooner on the lookout for original roots and original sin,
Leviathan of beginnings,
hunting whales breathing in the sea with lungs like
blood-surging forests,
relegated to dark and depth but forced always to return to
light and air.

His was a Greek love, nowhere domiciled, a dark-skinned
wayfarer with coils of wet greenery around his limbs,
     his truth was impossibility, his dream madness, a crying voice
from the fellowship of the damned:
     a dove seized by rage, oblivious of fear, and everything
magnified as at sunset,
     an ocean rider who cursed fire, with the white scar carved by
lightning's thrust along his body,
     rebelling against the elements, against the fatherhood of nature,
the god of snow, being all-powerful on its throne of skeletons,
     in a battle against the mountain of white myth, against the
slavery that left his hunger unsatiated, cannibalistic,
     an outcast among his sons, in fear of drowning, his sex eaten
by fish.

     Circling the world's navel, racing over the ocean, his life
existed before birth, not beyond death,
     but he gave in to the pressure, the traitor within him, the
grafted dread, the soured mother's milk,
     he betrayed his damnation, lost his truth, his ocean, his
darkness and his struggle,
     became the man who had gone ashore, brotherless, among
sisters disguised, forbidden, witches averting their sex,
     choked in this life, whitewashed with lime and snow,
     victim for a sacrificial offering, for a murdered brother
made divine by treason,
     and he lost his manly voice, a eunuch of silence,
     but wheels continued to crush horizons and thighbones
and distances were annihilated by fire that exploded in captivity.

The South: Louisiana

Railroads swallowed up by marshes of green:
deserted freight cars, burn spots on their floors,
the haunt of swarming wasps, tramps, homeless children.
Swaying in water and mud,
green clutches the ground and gasps for air,
phantoms of moss climb the blind trees to their death,
the woods still brood over the echoes of pirates' voices
and drink from the sea with cuttlefish roots
by beaches fluttering like poisoned eyelids,
by ragged-cotton shores,
by a sea without eyebrows and with forehead unlined.

From outlying rows of cabins and laundry
black women serving icewater emerge,
operating elevators in white gloves.
The canals are filled, the water dead
as the blood is dead, an overgrown depth
that neither mirrors black nor red,
between snow-filled baskets, between trees bursting into bloom,
into waving handkerchiefs or newly-slaughtered meat.

Frame houses sag under rusty fire escapes
behind trellises of roses and green wrought iron,
where female breasts bluer than sheep udders give suck
and drunken soldiers sing
between piles of crushed oranges.

Raw light bulbs kiss bottles
and chalky scrawled letters reel over mirrors;
in each bottle hides a rooster that burns and crows,
in each woman a mute river and a murdered mockingbird.

Small green sea horses ride in the tops of magnolias,
the mollusc-faces wait cool under their leafy hats
and from the eyes of alligators fall tears of tar.

Fires dig red cavities in the night,
the glare flickers across migrating blacks
with worn handbags and wrists like deer feet
in a soft whisper of naked soles against the stone.

Each man is king
with hunting rifle, cat-o'-nine-tails, watch fob, shoe cleats,
but the river has died under its concrete span,
bird song is stilled around the oil pools;
awaiting thunderbolts in their fight against pollution,
the long-legged watertanks
sit hunched up like spiders under the clouds;
doll-girls, their hips wrapped in silver net,
are waiting, their chinks open for dollars,
with kisses that seal worse than sealing-wax,
and kids on rollerskates whisk by like demons
chasing the newlyweds towing their string of tin cans.
But the honey from the wildflowers is gathered in darker
hair,
a honey that will burn in the throat forever
with the memory of shoulders bowed by the weight of buckets
and teeth that have bled under the anguish of kisses.

Landscapes reach out with straw and dust,
with the print of knees dug into the earth,
with rows of darkening cotton that the wind has swept together
and moss that comes with small quiet strangler hands
    while trees and fields call out of their captivity
through evenings when the stone has the soft fragrance of love.
    And she is a fish alive, a moist rose,
he, an awakening serpent, a nose that sniffs,
    and darkness covers their bodies with fireflies
that prick their skin with the needles of pleasure
    until their arms split amid the autumn harvest
and under a wet sky tin rooftops
are mirrored in buckets of water.

    The smell of burning human flesh
roams through the night like a mad dog.
Soot quivers on porcelain surfaces.
Sweat runs like melting shoe polish.
Snails hide in their shells.
The moon slides through meandering waters.
False asphodels cling to one's stomach;
cotton clothes hide frogs, quivering with cold.
    Blood-shot-eyed dogs drenched with dew
drivel over still-warm bones and aim for
an imagined pulse.

Van Gogh

Your rugged, bony face. Your green eyes.
A wave of silence where you passed.
Life's arms around your naked body,
Life's face beside yours.
You hungered with the starving;
Your hand rested on the hot heads of the sick.
The planets of your eyes shone in the soul's blackest alleys.

Who caressed *your* hot head?
Who calmed the storm in *your* heart?
Who hungered with *you*?
No one...
(A harlot, perhaps.)

Your soul—a torch of fire whisking and flickering in a storm.
Your heart—a wide restless ocean.
Sun-worshipper, sun-seeker finding your way through a blood haze.

We remember:
Your burning armfuls of sunflowers, sunflowers.
Your peculiar faces against deep-blue space and white nebulae.
Your wildly clenched fist, color spurting between your fingers,
Ground heaving in travail,
Trees writhing in wild longing toward the sun.
Black clouds enveloping fire-swirls.

Finally in your brain a sun: blazing, consuming, e x p l o d i n g.

Agadir

I was reading of the hunter Gracchus, whose coming was
     heralded by a dove on a windowsill
when a dove came to our terrace and gazed up at us, eyes
     big as pearls,
red and white-ringed.
Plump white seagulls often came to eat the crusts we
     threw to them, but never doves;
there by the sea they were shyer, unsteady on their
     shorter wings.
This one, long-necked, high-bosomed like a singer,
white, white, as if made of light snow,
seemed both surprised and terrified, as if faced with a
     difficult task,
mutely turned her head, displaying her beauty and
     her alarm,
leaving us to make her out as best we could:
What did she want to tell us? What message did she
     bring? A warning or a reproach?
That night we were oddly enough served fried pigeon for
     dinner; and
dined on it with guilt feelings and thought that we
     understood,
but, alas, the dove had intended more than just that !

*

The signs were everywhere, but we were blind like all
     the others.

The sky, a sky of ether and steel, was much too sharp
    a blue,
the sun was an open oven and the day a white stone
    licked by purple tongues,
the clouds came far too suddenly, low puffs of coal smoke
    over the ocean,
choking, but giving no rain.
Small white worms burst from the trees and sewed their
    black thread through the leaves,
beetles emerged from cracks in the earth and were
    lacquered blue or sprinkled with gold dust,
did not find what they sought and disappeared again.
Large ants assembled and together dropped their wings
    (which seemed made of glass),
a splinter hid beneath a nail, a pimple became inflamed
as if attempting to germinate,
beads of perspiration were pressed from crystals, an
    echo turned round
unable to answer, even cigarette lighters
refused to work . . .
Bird dung fell from the empty sky, glaring white, seeking
    some open eye to blind.

*

One morning the sea was black—
soil newly plowed
or fractured asphalt
rolling in heavy and greasy, black groundswells under
    silvery skeins of spit.
The depth of the sea turned up its muddy cheek (and in
    the mud there were star splinters).

The fishermen had their loaded nets sagging with dead
        sardines
(together with certain deep-sea fish, blood-shot, blown up
        into balls).
In the market patient hands arranged fish into
        silver wheels,
bristling chins scraped against nails and rubber soles
        sucked kisses from the cement floor,
auction bids were left hanging from the ceiling like
        long hooks.
Toward nightfall the sea, terrifyingly generous, delivered
        up a dead whale,
still bleeding profusely, rocking toward the shore like a
        capsized boat,
black, the rudder of its tail askew, as if in a field of
        poppies.
And the excited seabirds encircled it, screaming.

*

The first warning was a baby one,
an insignificant jolt,
as if a truck had passed, or the trees had rustled in a gust
        of wind:
only the dogs whimpered or barked, uneasy
in their ancient memories. And an opened newspaper
shivered, glasses clinked on trays, water sloshed in bowls,
        in basins,
the customers in bars laughed in a superior way, sure
        of themselves.
"And yet it moves!" the clever ones quoted (some even
        in Latin).

Well, the good earth could still shake and make herself felt;
it was almost like a reassurance of comfort and security:
they had, after all, everything on their side, the whole
     unshakable order that man had wrought over
     Nature,
protected by their technique, their science, their
     conveniences,
they held the power. (Catastrophes might well occur
     elsewhere,
but not here, not with them here.)
It was high noon, when man's confidence is at its peak.

*

The second warning was more serious, the child had
     grown to a young giant.
Again a warm day, too radiant, a desert heat of over
     ninety-five degrees on the twenty-ninth of
     February,
the leap-year day, the left-over day, the day for those
     who are left over, the day for old jokes.
Ramadan, the month of fasting, began with cracking gun
     shots.
At noon, ten minutes to twelve,
earth listed, shook, heavy and sickening,
for five seconds while we held our breath
and felt that we were traveling aboard the earth as on a
     ship;
the houses quaked like ships colliding,
glasses danced on the tables and fell to the floor,
     windowpanes shattered, plaster rained down.

Then silence, empty faces, eyes staring at each other;
many people rushed out, gazing up at space which was in
      no way involved,
bewildered, disoriented,
until confidence switched back, and voices and laughter
      rose stronger than they had been:
nothing could happen, one could feel completely safe,
and the day was beautiful, brilliantly clear, and there was
no danger at all in the world!

*

Waiting (who waited?) for letters for the pigeons and
      glances for the roses,
waiting for an attachment that had suddenly broken off,
      waiting for a hearth, for smoke, and joy for the animals,
waiting, waiting for repetitions that didn't take place and
      words that notebooks attracted like ants,
waiting (who waited?) for the avalanche that would
      empty the waiting room,
waiting for the murmur of the moon groves of dwarfed
      pine trees, oh, the murmur of the moon-lit pines,
waiting, waiting, why this waiting that would lead to nothing,
why this waiting filled only with itself and poorly
      prepared for anything else?
Waiting for a movement whose direction no one sensed
      anyway.

*

The night was clear and seemed without deceit.
A crescent moon, three nights and days old, set in the
      northwest,

the sea was calmer than usual, the heat had diminished,
the airplanes had ceased to stir up the sky and had come
      to rest for the night,
scattered groups of people were coming back from the
      movies
cigarettes glowed on the balconies,
under a palm tree on the Promenade a Moroccan and his
      wife were tardily saying their prayers,
and he was a bit ahead of her in his, and she followed his
      movements like a delayed shadow.
We had pulled down the iron shutter facing the terrace
      to a few feet from the floor,
and drawn the heavy yellow curtain: when the lights were
      off, the room was almost dark
except for a reflected ray of light in the wardrobe mirror
      opposite.
The anxiety left by the day's quake grew within me like a
      groundswell,
an unanswered question, a warning unheeded,
but I fell asleep on my right side, and the light swell
      calmed.

*

I heard myself cry out in sleep (I shall never know what
      I cried, never know if what I cried would have
      told me anything that I did not know)
at the very moment when I was thrown out of bed (or
      instinctively flung myself from it)
to curl up in a corner while the shock grew in
      overwhelming force,

becoming stronger and more violent,
coming from all directions at the same time, a rebellion
    from the entrails of the earth, a wild erupting dance,
a thunder from the depths, crushing in its weight,
smashing walls, cracking, collapsing.
No time to feel or think, nothing to do but wait like a
    mirror under a rain of stones,
and understanding that the foreboding had come true, that
    finally the end had come, was *now*,
that what had happened somehow already was part of the
    past while it still occurred,
everything came out like an equation that had been
    solved, an account added up and completed,
it did not come as a surprise, was no mistake, was as it
    had to be,
a closed circle.

*

Those seconds, longer than life,
each second containing birth and death,
trying to reveal your real self, show you your true face,
the face that no one sees, the secret that no one
    possesses, no sooner seen than lost again,
the moment of the curved mirror reflecting itself
and with the speed of light led through endless image
    after image,
image that was movement and stillness—endless,
    unfathomable,
beginning and ending and beginning again in itself, a
    spring imprisoned in its course,

and you were no one, a thin line dividing time from time,
your life was without importance in an endless
     combination,
everything was everywhere, balanced between the
     possible and the real,
all incredibly simple—before your moment trembled and
     fell,
like an ocean transformed into a drop of water, falling
     lower and lower and farther away.

*

How long did it last?
Ten seconds?
More? Less?
Or no time at all, time having ceased,
having lost its precise limits,
perhaps a dark ball of time compressed and loaded with
     decisions as swift as lightning,
for the world existed anew, immobile, silent;
conscience once again merged with the body; I was again
     alive
(or was it only an idea at the moment of death?)
and, as often in dreams, I groped for the light switch
     without being able to cut through the dark,
and I thought that I cried out in the dark and got an
     answer that confirmed that we were still alive,
I groped my way through rubble and debris toward the
     terrace door,
toward the crank, the metal shutter!
And we came out on the terrace;

the world still existed,
part of the building was still standing,
and we stood there barefoot among the rubbish,
in deathly silence, in darkness,
under the few stars.

*

He was a veteran of earthquakes,
standing there like a wooden statue, in his tight dressing
    gown, unlit pipe protruding from his long face;
I thought that he was English although he spoke French,
and he confirmed it, but in French, answering in French
    the questions I asked in English,
as if his true language, his mother tongue, had disappeared
    and only fragments of the language most recently
    used were left, floating on the surface.
This was his fourth major earthquake, he said, the three
    earlier ones having occurred in Turkey, Japan and
    New Zealand,
as if the quakes had followed him around the world and
    had tracked him down here:
each time he had survived with his pipe, without a scratch.
"But it's getting to be rather a bore," he said, suddenly
    regaining his mother tongue.
He began to tremble a while later, as we sat on the shore,
    huddled together back to back to keep warm.
I felt a back shivering continually against mine, a leaf in
    the wind, and the back was his, the veteran's;
he also made a tardy attempt to light his pipe, but his
    hands shook so that the match went out at once;

the shock reached him with a certain delay, through
      successive layers of paralysis,
the veteran of earthquakes.

*

Then the earth shook again, deep shudders swept
      through the ground
dogs howled at length to one another from all sides, and
      a muted
wailing arose from the human multitudes.
Some kept breathlessly still,
others who had been sitting stretched out on the ground,
while others sprawling on the ground got up.
Indeed, everything now depended on the earth's
      capriciousness, its
indifference or fury:
Would it quake and twist itself in a wild dream of
      unknown torments?
Or would it once again fall to rest, sink into oblivion?
Was it old or young? Was it late or early? An end or yet a
      beginning?
In the harbor a fire flared up and raged, lighting up its
      own smoke swirling into the sky;
the crowd on the ground was lit up repeatedly by passing
      headlights,
and dense rows of faces stared as in a movie house, in
      rapt attention at all that was happening;
the wounded bled on the ground, gently moaning, and
      others vomited quietly where they lay,
buses began to make their rounds, picking up the injured,
      lifting them from the dark throng,

59

with sudden bright bursts of red blood, that struck us as
      very strange.

*

Shipwrecks not at sea but ashore,
terra firma heaving like the sea;
houses had foundered like ships in petrified waves,
Talborj, the white city, the Moroccans' densely populated
      quarter,
was entirely in ruins, as if it had gone through a giant mill,
and dust had settled like flour everywhere and
      shipwrecked souls staggered about
like mummies risen out of the accumulated dust of
      millennia, stirring up white dust as they moved,
with the dust rust-stained with blood, stamped with blood
      as with sealing wax on white paper,
and the dead lay there as if unearthed from a lime pit,
their hair seemingly cut out of white stone above faces
      masked in plaster;
dogs roamed about like white ghosts, ashamed,
rats wandered around in the sun, shameless,
trees were white and seemed dead, giving off puffs of
      smoke with each gust of wind,
water kept running under a film of white too tough to
      break,
children wept quietly, digging with their fists ever darker
      furrows around their eyes
in the utter whiteness of their faces.

*

Machines began to arrive, steam shovels, drilling
     machines,
together with specialists, rescue workers, soldiers,
come to take over the city, fight against death and ruins,
guardsmen with their guns at the ready, outdoor kitchens
     with soup and bread, medicine cabinets wide open,
stretchers to carry away the dead and line them up along
     the edge of the roads,
the dead lined up to be viewed and identified, with the
     faces of peace or horror, or even with no faces at all,
awaiting mass graves and quicklime, already attracting
     rats and blue flies.
There were also those in despair who did not give in, who
     fought against the heaps of ruins with their bare
     hands,
and those who had been rescued smoking their first
     cigarette by the edge of the grave they had
     risen from,
and the famished who had refused to eat anything
     before nightfall because it was Ramadan,
and the girl who had been unable to prevent her younger
     brother from chewing on her arm,
and the man who, pulling his wife by her hair, found
     himself holding her severed head in his hands,
and the man who had his leg cut off with a hacksaw and
     left it behind between two stone blocks,
and children who suddenly smiled again, so exhilarating
     and so awful to see.

*

"Just as I plunged into the dark I felt that God existed,
I was seized with terror and joy: God made his presence
        known,
demonstrated his power over the world, showed that
        against God there is no relief except in God,
no buildings, no walls, no inventions or machines mean
        anything to God,
He sets the depths trembling and all our security is
        broken down like straw,
His will alone upholds all that exists, invades everything,
        more omnipresent than water and air.
What a mistake to search for Him when He is already
        part of everything, when He already envelops and
        sinks into us,
we have only to let ourselves go, and not want anything
        beyond His will,
God has the same absolute love for all,
for me whom He permitted to survive, whom He filled
        with the certainty of His presence,
for all those who had died at the time of the catastrophe,
        joyfully united with Him,
for all those who still hover between life and death,
        imprisoned in the ruins,
those to whom He has given the time to know and to
        change."

*

"We had just come back from the movies;
my wife had not liked the film and took a warm bath to
        forget it, so that she might sleep.
I read the paper waiting for her, the door of the bathroom
        stood a little ajar, and I heard the sound of the
        water when she moved in her tub,
then the light blinked and disappeared in a hurricane of
        crumbling walls and ceilings,
and I fell as in a plunging elevator, down into space, into
        the void.
Not knowing what had happened, I awoke half-conscious
        in the dark,
and when they dug us out, I still held the paper crumpled
        up in my hand,
my wife was still in the tub, which had not overturned
        or even lost much water,
she floated there naked and unharmed, but dead,
drowned, her fair flowing in a blonde swirl around
        her face.
Shall I now thank God for my salvation?"

*

"My wedding day, and I a fifteen-year-old bride
from far up in the mountains, and I had never before seen
        the sea and so many huge buildings . . .
We sat around the wedding feast: everything shone and
        hovered around me, as in a dream;
my bridegroom sat there by my side, alien and stern, like
        the wild briar, ready to draw my blood.

63

He would liberate me from the childhood that enveloped
      me like a bandage, and I had a tingling sensation
      all over;
he let me hold his hand between courses this wedding
      night, but I understood it would never become
      a habit.
Then the world began to shake and everything broke
      down around us;
I held on to his hand and we plunged down into the dark
      as into a well, in a dizziness that might
      be happiness,
it had to turn out that way, could not be any other way,
      I understood.
There was too little time and my wedding night fell into
      darkness all too fast.
But I awoke once again somewhere, to darkness and
      silence and I held fast to his hand,
something rested over me, like a wooden slide, that I
      could not move,
and I did not know where he was, but soon his hand
      began to feel cool in mine and did not answer
      when I squeezed it;
then I screamed and understood: I had survived, alone
      under a bed that was crushing me,
a little fifteen-year-old widow, my real life having lasted
      only one night."

*

"Words also crumbled, broke into pieces, scattered in
      shreds,

in vain I tried to find some still unharmed and usable
but found only splinters of metaphors, cracked, like a
        split mirror;
visions floated about, islands adrift in air as white as milk
        but thicker,
almost like molten, viscous marble,
trees floated about, torn up by the roots and turning
        slowly upside down upon themselves,
people floated like driftwood, many whole and outwardly
        unmarred, others cut in half or worse,
floating about in the white with eyes wide open, hair
        streaming upward,
the whole scene spotless and beautiful, like a devastation
        of statues,
black tabletops turned slowly, became round holes of dark
        tapering into a streak,
horses floated on their backs, legs galloped in the void,
so many things went by: sandals two by two as if held
        together by invisible feet, bolts of cloth unrolling,
a sidewalk cafe filled with people leaning over an abyss,
a fire burning in the void, a sports car filled with
        young girls,
and whether I closed my eyes or kept them open made no
        difference; the sights were there inside,
my brain was stripped of words, white and blank,
only images floated around there after the breakdown."

*

Death's city would now lie there, behind its barriers, with
        its whitewashed ruins, ghost white,

the stench of death would penetrate everything, the
        nauseous odor
of putrefaction like an invisible smoke around the ruins,
the rats and flies and all the vermin would gather there
        forthwith,
a swarming, crawling multitude,
vultures would come from nowhere, black, raising dust,
        they would await their hour,
cats and dogs would quickly go wild from hunger and
        homelessness and degenerate into eaters
        of carcasses,
they would be shot and lie there stretched out on the
        ground, their hair already stiff and lustreless,
the rescue party would stride around in their white
        sanitary masks like beings from another planet,
seeking a hidden life in Death's city:
for there would always be a last resort on the scale, a
        shelf of possibility,
where lives would be preserved like fragrances locked up
        in flagons, delicate, yet enduring,
and they would constantly search in the eerie silence of
        the stones until all hope had expired,
would listen with their ears to the stones, seeking the least
        sound from the thinnest crack,
but the stones would in the end be mute, without a sigh,
graves forever guarding their secrets.

*

What did we know about roots that had tied themselves
        into a deadly knot?
What did we know about moles suffocated in their tunnels?

What did we know about the tremors under the donkey's
      skin?
What did we know of the fissures where light had been
      petrified like glass?
What did we know of hands that would not let go of each
      other until dissolved in water or mud?
What were we other than forms of clay that evaded our
      moment of truth?
But the dumb ruins would find a voice and begin to
      whisper,
the stones would bear witness for the lives of men to
      come,
ravens would bring sorrow to the mountains,
from the sea, seagulls would come with hope,
wild poppies would come with traces of blood and the
      lustre of flame,
the briar would come and the winged singers seeking
      shelter in the thorny thicket,
and flame would come to the briar and rain to the flame,
and a white dove might once again perhaps come to
      a window in warning
or to proclaim life's joy, earth's peace.

*

The plane sped forward and took off from this shaken
      ground,
ascended into the dense air free of fissures, into untouched
      space,
and reeled off over the bay with the dead city askew,
      balancing down below

67

on the world aslant, still white, still beautiful in its
       desolation,
its own extended funeral monument:
AGADIR!
Name tremblingly engraved on our hearts and skin,
Agadir, ten seconds and never more,
Agadir, farewell!
We fled from you, refugees and strangers,
we who had no roots in your fate,
we who had plucked our lives like firebrands from the fire
       and escaped:
your desolation we left behind us like blowing ashes,
brought with us horror like a fresh memory, a black abyss
       or whitening scar,
together with the pride over what we had survived, lived
       through,
heroes for one day, facing flashbulbs and the press,
without responsibility like whirling chaff, flying away with
       our risked and rescued lives.

*

But the relief counterbalanced the shame, a feeling
that bled somewhere within us, a bitter powerlessness,
       a reproach
of betrayal: Agadir's demands
for us to be loyal in the disaster, to suffer with the
       suffering, joining in its fate.
These seconds, minutes, hours that welded us together with
       plunging rocks and fissured ground,
Agadir, never more,

Agadir, forever within us, white city of life and death, life
    clasped by death,
Agadir, already sunk into the past, forever a mirage before
    our inner eye,
Agadir,
be ready, remember
what is perhaps in store for us: the greater destruction,
 a world in ruins, earth laid waste, only Death trailing
    smoke and disappearing into space,
never more,
forever,
Agadir.

Kjell Hjern
(1916–1984)

Kjell Hjern spent his entire life as a free-lance writer in his native Gothenburg. His interest in the history of the city is well documented in his books about the Gothenburg Arts Society over a period of a hundred years (1954); Theater at Götaplatsen (1964); photo-books from Gothenburg, a history of the Valand Art School (1972); and others, for which the University of Gothenburg rewarded him with an honorary doctorate.

Hjern was editor of the art magazine *Paletten*, 1941–47, and served as the art and theater critic of the liberal *GHT*, 1946–49. He was theater critic of *Ord och Bild*, 1950–61, and literary critic at the Gothenburg paper *GP*, 1959–65.

His debut, *Måspredikan* (Seagull's Sermon, 1948) was followed by *Ögonblick med jorden* (Moments with the Earth, 1954), and *Den eviga glädjens palats* (The Palace of Eternal Joy, translations of Chinese poetry, 1958). Hjern also published a number of anthologies. A selection of his poetry, *Ett decennium, Dikter 1949–59* (A Decade, Poems 1949–59) appeared in 1963 and *Kustremsa* (Coastal Fringe) was published in 1978.

At times Hjern maintained rather intense contacts with the Scandinavian writers he admired. As a young man he appreciated, and was later in touch with, some of the most outstanding modernists in Finland: Björling, Parland, Diktonius, and Enckell, all of whom wrote in Swedish.

It is not easy to characterize Hjern. One critic described him as a cynic. Göran O. Eriksson called him "an awkward writer."

Hjern became something of a poet of compassion, but there was no risk that he would ever become sentimental as long as he remembered his own dictum: "One's own compassion one should direct toward people who can take it." At the same time he felt that it would be a mistake to expect any large portions of sympathy, even when they might be appropriate. On the other hand one has certain mechanisms at one's disposal, of course. One can call someone a "fool" who was too stingy to give a little comfort or sympathy. "But it's no use admitting your shortcomings to a fool, for he will literally take you at your word."

If the combination—too strong a sensitivity and a fear of death—prevails, it can lead to borderline experiences in which the dream is hard to separate from reality. Hjern intimates that that is the case in the poem "Autumnal Landscape," in which two old men intensely discuss the rather subtle question of whether the chow dog has gray or brown eyes. Is everything contradictory, relative, uncertain, subjective? At any rate their discussion provides the wanderer-poet a "momentary tranquility of mind."

In his villa Hjern surrounded himself with books, preferably first or leather-bound editions, pictures, and music. Everything was neatly and attractively arranged. Hjern was a great storyteller—with a tremendous memory—who also in his poems effectively displayed his knowledge of people and insights into human psychology.

Hjern's themes vary from the large to the small, the everyday to the unique, the personal to the impersonal, the local to the universal. An evening walk to a look-out point near his villa would suffice to set him pondering his own life's wandering and perhaps even eternal questions. When he termed his homey feeling for life entirely "absurd," it was his way of confessing how thoroughly "uncertain" life appeared to him. He probably used "absurd" in the sense that the mystics used the term. Hjern's elegant, finely wrought style, and his undeniable humor, add to his appeal. This is the first time any of his poems have been translated into English.

On Discovering the Importance
of a Garden Seat

The lily pond lay sleeping amid the dark cavernous shrubbery and the goldfish I had gone out to see were invisible. I turned my eyes toward the heavens and began at once with drunken determination to count the stars. Staring upward, I reeled back and forth on the gravel path and became drunker and drunker. After a while my knee knocked against a garden seat, the importance of which I promptly discovered. Startled and proud of my discovery, I crawled in under it and the slot between the two planks of the seat limited my field of vision pleasantly. Thus I counted up to twelve stars and fell asleep with a feeling that I too would little by little be able to play a significant role in my community.

To My Love

You have as many defects as a pig has lice and you will rub against me in vain to get rid of them. Your dishonesty is as great as your reputation for honesty, which is also great. I alone know you, my love, and know your measurements and sing your praises in true poetry. Perhaps there are women who are more beautiful than you and who lie less often, but I do not want to exchange you for any of them if I do not have to. Like the pig, you are good throughout, and as long as I am in my right mind, I shall love you with a great and insatiable appetite.

Between Book Lovers

Once I felt remorse because of a book, which I had come by in the way that book lovers often do. When I later came across a passage in which the author states that words of truth and reason belong just as much to the one who first uttered them as to the one who repeats them and noticed the question mark with which the former owner had smudged the page, I felt that my right to ownership had been strengthened even more.

The Price of Stability

It is with a wonderful sense of security that for the past several days I can climb upon the chair by the farthest bookcase thanks to the mending of its fourth leg, which my carpenter brothers have completed. The chair's security is a great joy to me and were it not that because of it I so often forget why I have stepped up on the chair, I would just for the pleasure of getting it repaired smash all the rest of my furniture to smithereens.

Meaning to Life

I feel lonely and deserted by God and man and hopelessness is not far away. Then I suddenly remember that I have a pair of shoes to pick up at the shoemaker's, for which he has been waiting more than a month to be paid. My depression has vanished into thin air and I discover that there is still some meaning to life.

In the Big City

Loneliness depressed me in the restaurant where I had looked in vain for a familiar face, and I ordered a steak with garlic butter. The splendid dish tempered my melancholia and the garlic made my feeling of desolation evaporate; the taste followed me the rest of the day and when I sank at night into my cool bed, I still had company, which over and over made its presence felt.

Cultivated Ground

When young, one is fearful of being influenced by other writers. With maturity that fear dissipates and one detects the sound of foreign voices on one's home ground and is often delighted to be helped with a few thrusts of the spade. It is more important that the earth be properly cultivated than that every potato be planted with a jerk of the arm uniquely one's own.

On the Growth of Hair in Middle Age

No poem has yet been written
except possibly in Chinese
about the growth of hair that occurs
during a man's best years
when the hair on his head has begun to thin.

The hair then growing from the nose
can more readily be tolerated
when a man sports a full beard,
but even then it gets in the way
if the cathedral of the nose
has delicate walls.

For this is not just innocent fluff
as on a bald pate
when it tries to deny the aging process.
No, these hairs are like lances,
unfavorably disposed one toward the other.

And when you wish to remove them,
they stick together;
and you are left cursing those miserable tools,
tweezers with warped shanks.

There are, to be sure, bold blades
that seize the nose hairs by the end
and quickly yank them out,

blades that may be compared to those
that operate farther down to snip out the appendix,
which, incidentally, needs to be done but once,
while nose hair returns again and again.

Here Science,
which otherwise horses about,
asking in that self-important way,
"What can I do for you?
May I help you?"
has shamefully failed;
and Poetry,
the pompous winged mare,
patronizingly turns her rump on us
when we attempt to re-create
these wretched scenes of everyday life.

Östen Sjöstrand
(1925–   )

Östen Sjöstrand, born in Gothenburg, as a young man converted to Roman Catholicism. His literary roots are in the Swedish and European poetry of the 1940s.

Because of its mystical nature and the symbolic world that it evokes, his poetry is difficult but rewarding. Take, for instance, the short poem "Madrigal":

> Night came down, and the disease struck me with silence,
> paralyzed my eye and my foot
> it paralyzed my eye and my foot.
>
> The doctor came, and the doctor said to me:
> for this night there is no antidote
> there is no antidote.
>
> Passion came and passion said to me:
> night can hide your soul, your root
> but it cannot hide—a spark
> —that spark resides in your innermost room
> —and flares, beyond the night.

Even apart from formal consideration—such as number of lines and rhyme scheme—Östen Sjöstrand's "Madrigal" is unusual: it requires an extremely close reading to determine what is said and implied in these few lines.

A madrigal is a short love poem. But what kind of love is the poet here referring to? These are the gloomy night thoughts of the persona of a suffering, handicapped poet. There is darkness all around him during the night, his vision is impaired and his visibility reduced. The attending physician, who cares for the body, offers no cure. Physical love, "a spark of nature's fire" (Burns), a temporary vital energy that comes next, can make him forget his being, even his origin, but it has no effect on the spark within, which flickers "beyond the night," literally "outside of night."

If the ordinary spark provides merely partial illumination in the darkness, it has the potential to kindle a flame and develop into fuller light, dawn, or daylight. Yet we think of a spark as something fickle, unsteady, impermanent. Here it flickers "beyond the night," i.e., during day as well as night, perhaps prior to life and even in the ultimate darkness, death. If the reader associates this with the "life spark of celestial fire, called conscience" that George Washington spoke of, it is even more tempting to go one step further in interpretation. We can postulate the existence of a spark that operates on its own, independently of the person. If so, the spark would have to be kindled by divine rather than magic forces; this in its turn assumes a number of beliefs, in ulterior, perhaps even irresistible, grace, a life after death, and so on. Then the love expressed in this madrigal would also entail the love of God, which by definition involves the love of self, and of neighbor.

Even in many of his early travel poems spiritual reality tends to assert itself: Sjöstrand's later poetry is in the tradition of Valéry and Eliot and moves back and forth in time, as if simultaneity were a fact. Musicality is a strong element in Sjöstrand's poetry. He also translated Auden's text to Stravinsky's *The Rake's Progress* into Swedish (1961) and wrote the musical drama *Gästabudet* (The Banquet, 1962) in collaboration with the composer Sven-Erik Bäck.

Sjöstrand's orientation has been primarily French; he translated an anthology of French poetry in 1969. Among his other books of translation are works by Yves Bonnefoy (1971), Alain Bosquet (1981), Yannis Ritsos (with T. Kallifatides, 1971), and Wole Soyinka (1983).

As a counterpart to Sjöstrand's religious poetry, his interest in and knowledge of the natural sciences is much in evidence in "Cloud upon Cloud" in *De Gåfulla Hindren* (The enigmatic obstacles, 1961).

Sjöstrand's books of literary essays include *Världen Skapas Varje Dag* (The world is created every day, 1960), and *Fantasiens Nödvändighet* (The necessity of imagination, 1971).

A critical study *Östen Sjöstrand* by Staffan Bergsten (Twayne's World Authors Series, No. 150) appeared in 1974. Sjöstrand served for thirteen years as the editor of the review *Artes*, sponsored by the Swedish Academy, of which he is a member, as he is of the Academy of Music and Royal Academy of Art, Stockholm. As editor, he introduced his readers to many American authors, among them, Joyce Carol Oates, William Jay Smith, and Frederick Morgan.

The Remote Lunar Light of Memory

The remote lunar light of memory
shades the room with images:
the columns of the Acropolis as white as snow—

The point of a needle shines
like fish scales near the airy film of the sea.

In Principio

In the beginning—
In the beginning—

when the earth was cold or warm
(only because it was moving)

In the beginning—
In the beginning—

before stone was polished
before hands reached up to green

In the beginning—
In the beginning—

before protection suits were needed
against virus clouds and fire

In the beginning—

before protecting and enclosing walls
were raised—

long before all encircling walls
        ramparts
        breastworks
        barriers
long before walls, brick walls, dividing

before stone steel and concrete
    split apart
    exploded
    burst in two

before human beings became aware of one another
    for the first time—

before all deserts, all wilderness, all ruined
    places of refuge—

before the staggering night-blind steps toward houses
toward cities, rising from ashes—
    toward borders, toward frontiers
    reeking with corpses...

    In the beginning
    there was no one
    except you—

Solitary stars—
a common horizon.

Cloud Upon Cloud

Cloud upon cloud
of underground fire—
Extermination clouds
of hatred and abstraction—
And we who live still breathe
in the memory of another life.
But this is our life:
strontium and disgust.
And the hidden contagion
that is spreading, that already has penetrated us,
cut us off from ourselves, severed
hands from head, body and sex
from the heart, man from woman
as East from West—

Cloud upon cloud—

What a miracle that this world within the world
still emits its bright rays,
that womb, breasts, lips
still catch their weak echo
and that our eyes can still find
the secret motive
of another life.
But this is our life: strontium and disgust.
Cesium and emptiness.
Compact, compressed rock sealing in
hate against hate.
Space that does not breathe,

unchanging space.

Trees, animals wither away as we do
in this abandoned land—

Cloud upon cloud
of underground fire—
Extermination clouds
of hatred and abstraction—
This is our life
while ash keeps falling falling. . . .

X-ray Picture

He saw a park bench broken in two by a large rock. Not completely in two, for the two halves still hung together. He tried to bend them back, to fit the splintered parts together again, and return the bench intact to its place in the spruce grove. But it was as if the bench pursued an inner resistance of its own. Reluctantly he withdrew across the lawn—

And the hammer is lifted against the Greek urn: the microfilms of runways and mountain hangars are handed over at the secret meeting place; the bed is made up again—and without a sound, with a soft ball stuffed into his mouth, he falls flat on his face in the hallway, pursued to the very end by a savage pack of dogs he had once taught to hunt.

Memory Image

She held the little boy by the hand and led him toward me. They were both naked, but the woman was wearing a strange Phrygian silver cap. I was struck by how freely the child moved, and how independent he seemed. (Outwardly he resembled the young acrobat painted by Picasso.)

Then, I thought, the terrible destructive planetary cloud has not doomed me to be forever childless. But the boy's face did not belong to me but to other parents.

The woman, seeing that I was in a state of near exhaustion, pointed at a mountain. Was she pointing to a tomb amid rocks, meaning for me to make a pilgrimage to it? But I was so weary that such a journey was possible only in thought.

But I stopped thinking about myself. And I saw at the same time that the rock was split through and that the boy had emerged from the rock: that he had been there from the beginning.

I got up from my chair, climbed the stair, extending my hand to her whom I loved from the depth of all time. Together we strolled off to the kitchen. The day was not yet over. And soon in the late dawn wind the night's shadows would disperse.

On the Outermost Edge

I

On the outermost edge of the ocean,
where the vessels of confidence have foundered,
where will and resolve have
split in two
like rib and rudder,
and the heart has lost all its stabilizers,
there I beheld you,
you who seek us out,
you who force us beyond all limits,
beyond water and earth,
beyond the visible,
into silence.

II

In the body's innermost darkness,
where once the heavens sang,
but now have become silent
in a devastated open country
and the pulse beats as in an animal
that suddenly knows
it bears the light within itself,
there I beheld you,
you who seek us out,
you who force us beyond all limits,
beyond the visible,
into silence.

III

Terror pulls a roof of tin over itself
as protection against the ravaging fire.

Up from crumbling stone floors, from ruptured earth,
which the horizon will never again protect,
rose the vapor of Nothingness

and I heard all that is mute,

a people which has lost its language
and lost its way in the desert of emptiness.

IV

I heard all that is mute,

but the mute
was not the outermost nor the innermost boundary.

I shall speak once more,
in a language that is preserved
in words that once more stretch their roots
in a soil which the dead,
Nothingness itself has fertilized.

And where memory's wintry traces long ago have been erased,
you shall speak, you the Unknown One,
not of that which is beginning or ending,
but of that which is being.

V

And the stones are glowing.
And the water pulsates.
And the mountains fold,
and move slowly
toward the earth's poles,
toward the earth's deserts—
even toward a sea meadow
in northern Europe,
where the thawing lays bare
new words of creation
and trust.

You follow us,
you with the unknown features,
through the darkness of the living,
toward the star, which alone shimmers
in black air.

95

Hamlet in Dubrovnik

Down there the breakers hollow out the limestone.
Up here, atop the fortress
Fortinbras has saluted the dead prince
and the new state.
The folds of chain and chain cables
still wail
with human sorrow. Yes, in the spray
of the jesters' rolling web
treason and evil passions
were clear-cut masks. But in the fortress courtyard
beneath the arches
(where darkness has been notched by the torches of life's little hour),
people have gone astray and got lost in their roles:
they share the uncertainty and agony of the prince
so intent upon his retribution. (But he alone
maintains his balance
on the treacherously smooth stones of the castle courtyard.)

Up here the martial music has stopped.
The cannon smoke drifts off in the night wind.
On the fortress wall
the challenge of flowering broom, renewed desire,
injustice and fatalism.

Act of Faith

Glacial winters, heat waves,
floods, droughts,
clouds that drive westward
and southward, closely observed
by the organizers of Pestilence . . .

Yes, indeed, even I have fought against an Aztec god
ravaging all with his vividly ice-blue
geranium sheen,
     and I have renewed my vow
to Poetry!
    The sparkling water by the rock
does not quiet down.

It is with us that everything lives, everything dies.

Lake Tserknitsa
(Slovenia)

For months
dry, fertile soil,
where peasants sweat under straw hats
and noon slumbers beside growing ears
and cooling jugs.

On trucks and creaking ox carts the dry harvest is piled—
before pools warn of
flooding, the water of the lower regions, the lake
which for months will mirror a dead calm
or bend in waves before the north wind's furious stone thrusts.

Months of waiting—
for the opposite to arrive.

Herzegnovi: In the Midday Sun

I have been here before.
In the midday heat I climbed the steep alleyway
among citrus trees and agave,
among Hotel Boka's heavy palms,
I felt the pull of a divine Gestalt:
myrrh,
and the rustle of white cool silk.
But behind closed shutters
the shadows of the past,
battling to settle accounts,
pulled dagger and sword in rage:
I saw a scimitar around the sun!

    Uncertain about the road
I linger now in the warm shade.
But the red bougainvillaea,
clinging to the warm walls,
hides no nostalgia. The present is you.
And beyond the Spanjola fortress,
the Turkish belltower,
history is a lingering haze
above the blinding surface of the sea,
a friendly hum from the harbor.

The flowers of truth open up toward evening.

I do not fear them.

Among red midday flowers,
by the red-violet bougainvillaea,
you are with me, close, close.

On a swift runner's legs
you suddenly race toward me—
I feel your warm thighs
around my hips—

And I take you,
positive of the roots of growth,
certain of the strong colors
that bloom in the midday heat
closest
to the dazzling
dark—

we venture that rare thing:
the *now*.

To Eva

From Östen

At the moment when numbness and paralysis gave way

Your nakedness is hidden among the luminous autumn leaves
among the tree trunks of the forest, which, with lifted limbs,
move swiftly, dancing in a ring
with their red-yellow, coquettish skirts.

Your nakedness quivers close to me
where tears rise in thin capillary vessels
but will never gather in a flask at my wrist.

I touch your bare arms, your wrists,
when we go together toward the fresh glades amid pine and rowan
    trees,
where no withering will threaten,
and the earth, even on the darkest winter night,
will continue to stand forth in all its glory.

I feel your naked hips move beside me
when we saunter downhill
where the green twigs of blueberries and ligonberries have the
    fragrance of your hair.

Your ample breasts press against my shoulder blades,
when on high cliffs,
we gaze out over a life
that quivers just below the tree tops.
Even if I wander about in an unreal, subterranean Trojan labyrinth

which still has a visible exit, a central stairway,
I will, in the middle of my life, still cry out:

In this light only *you* exist.

When we take each other in our arms,
and our naked senses, our heads are almost one,
are one in the kiss,
let no despondency obscure
what deep feeling has said, and says.
And no exhaustion can silence it,
although people and landscape appear to keep silent
in all directions.

All I need do is turn some distance away
from the ticking time that is yours and mine
and the never obvious day repeats:
It is true,
it is true,
and you exist, you are real.

New clouds, and new energy gather.
I walk more calmly, even if at times alone, at your side.
I have found just now that your hand and your fingers
do not respond instantly to mine.
And with your whole naked being you are with me
by the sparkling fjord,
where the bridge's iron railing cries out with gloom,
but the sun, uncovered and indestructible, shines.

Springlike creature in this fluid room of the world,
so filled with sorrow and with so many yet unborn,
do not in hesitation or distrust
lift your hand to your forehead.

With body lying red and full
here beside you,
I will not, from lingering sorrow
nor from the contagious virus of indolence,
bury my face in my hands.

Let my deep feeling speak freely,
as freely as the water that murmurs in the mountain brooks
beside which we recently have walked.

There exists a closeness in which the autumn wind
is transformed into an open and undisguised cry,
which echoes take up over and over:
I will be there,
beloved, dearest one, the cry goes.

No charged silence can stifle that cry.

But I feel you unwinding the thread on a ball,
thread that draws me out of the deepest dark where
I've been forced to combat *my* bullheaded human-bodied monster
I feel your sudden and cautious hand
as I have felt it against my shoulder on awaking.

Do not be afraid when lightning in the recovered day,
reborn alertness as in slumber,
speaks its dazzling, undisguised, plain language.

It speaks with my voice, says in my poor language:
I will appear. I will be there.

Folke Isaksson
(*1927–*   )

Folke Isaksson was born at Kalix, northern Sweden, the son of a missionary priest with whom he did not get on entirely well, as several of his poems attest. Isaksson was raised in the old towns of Kalix and Gammelstad. He studied Nordic literature and languages and comparative literature at the University of Uppsala for a few years before he became a successful, and rather romantic, poet, who made a living as a reviewer for Stockholm newspapers.

His *Vinterresa* (Winter tour, 1951) was clearly influenced by Rilke. Even Rilke's angel had a place in it. *Det gröna året* contains some wonderful portraits: Master Linnaeus; Doctor Serafica; Dylan Thomas, and one of "The Bumblebee," which begins:

> Murmuring little bear it flies across in its wood,
> talks to itself with a mouth full of sugar.
> Clicking its tongue, yawning in its palm,
> it will soon prepare its winter lair in the sweet hay.
> Hark, how it snores now in its bed!

Clearly the poet does not want to compete with entomologists; he is quite content to soar, *docere et delectare,* in this poem. *Det Gröna året* may be seen as a breakthrough for Isaksson. *Blått och svart* (Blue and Black, 1957) contains "Linnaeus at Work on Nemesis Divina," "A Poet in Connecticut" (Wallace Stevens), "The Owl,"

"The Scream" (Francis Bacon), and refers to one of Isaksson's favorites, the poet Almqvist (1793–1866), as does also *Teckenspråk* (Sign Language, 1959). With *Terra magica* (Magic land, 1963) a change takes place, for this book contains one of his first political poems of the 1960s. From the very beginning Isaksson had always experienced a conflict between his social conscience and his tendency to idealize. Notable is the poem "Torture," which ends:

> There is morning, they have sought a light
> They punish her for her treachery. They have
> torn apart her waist
>
> There is morning, there is forenoon
> and like children they sleep.

Terra magica also includes a poem about Tiresias visiting the concentration camp at Theresienstadt near Prague.

The conflict he experienced grew to the point that production of poetry became virtually impossible and thus ceased until 1981. "I was a lyric poet," he wrote in 1983, "who, after five books of poetry and a couple of translations, went silent. In the handbooks I could soon detect that I belonged to the society of used-up poets. I stopped writing my own poetry and also stopped reading the poetry of others."

From the mid-1960s on he had been beset by a feeling that poetry was a morally ineffectual enterprise (one recalls W. H. Auden's lament that his poetry had failed to save the life of a single Jew during the Holocaust); it was "something soft and pleasing, but not quite necessary." Scarcely wishing to give up writing itself, Isaksson took off for India and other countries to pursue socio-political commentary and to compose travel books.

A substantial collection of new poems, *Tecken och under* (Signs and wonders, 1981), was a complete critical success. Isaksson further reaffirmed his commitment to the poetic enterprise by means of his impressive volume of criticism, *Gnistor under himlavalvet* (Sparks beneath the vault of heaven, 1983), which opens with his contemplative proclamation of a "Return to Poetry." The book offers twenty-five evaluations of poets from Marvell and Blake to Bertrand and Baudelaire, Auden and Cavafy, as well as such Swedish masters as Stagnelius, Södergran, Aspenström, Eva Runefelt, and many others.

In recent years Isaksoon has published *Vingslag* (Wingbeats, 1986) and the selected poems of *Vindens hand* (The hand of the wind, 1988). His early translations of Wallace Stevens (1957) have now been followed by one of Blake's *Marriage of Heaven and Hell* (1988); also in recent years, he has collaborated with Bela Javorsky on translating two volumes of the Hungarian poet Sándor Csoori. The latter have led to Swedish television features, entrusted to Isaksson and the producer and poet Christian Stannow, offering a personal view of the present state of poetry in Hungary and in the United States.

Isaksson's books of prose poems are *Skiftningar i en väv* (Tinges on a web, 1985) and *Ombord på Skymningsexpressen* (On board the twilight express, 1988). They range from recollections of childhood and siftings through dreamlike scenes of travel to essays of mature experience on a variety of subjects. Isaksson's *Collected Poems 1951–1986* appeared in 1988 (FIB). With Olov Isaksson, his brother, he published an excellent history of his old hometown, *Gammelstad—500 Years* in 1992.

The Owl

Behind his feigned blindness
he ponders life.
The farmer goes to the well.
A shiver swims across the fields.
Evening comes on slowly,
a wing-beat.
Shrunk into his sloth,
the owl watches the village disappear,
fade out with the farmer and the well.
A gray twilight film numbs the world.
A bell rings inside a mitten.
Then he releases his grip,
brushes against the well-sweep,
and strikes his claws into the weathercock of the church.
He sharpens his beak against the gold:
Night screams with sparks.

The Carpenter
on the Finnish poet Elmer Diktonius

He scrutinizes the wood. The tough, tender look:
and in the grain the twig's eye.

On the threshold he stands, lifting the jack-plane,
catching on its cutting edge the sun-smile.
Sputters, tightens his grip, begins.

The wood bristles and spits like an old tomcat.

See how he smiles then in that twig's eye of his
when the obstinate coarse shavings
begin to twitch and swagger across the floor,
exploding in curses.

The moths of twilight fill the shed.

The Sea in My Words

The sea is always in my words
in my blood in my breath
in these tired sad eyes
I who never saw the sea
was never rocked to sleep
by a pounding wave
I who saw only strips and edges of the sea
coasts gleaming from a
distance plains crocheted with gulls
a solitary brig on the rim of morning
the boatlike island with the beacon
(heading toward deeper expanses
dawn over a snow-crust over eel-colored lowlands
over the freedom the pitiless indifferent oblivion of the sea)

I who have not seen the sea
hear the roar of the surf and the delirious joy
as murmuring seashells are heard on sandy paths
memories of broken masts and sudden death
of scurvy and despair in the clutch of the autumn storm

I who have not seen the sea
am myself closest to the sea
island or rock pointer or portent
reaching out to thought and hand
I am myself cape island or eye
shrouded by the smoke and thunder of the storm
by its intimacy and its abandon

(Now a memory: the leer of the wind
one day in icy sunlight men at the prow
a ship crossed ours
coil of smoke against smoke
that rose into the void
of voyage and venture
of storm and stillness
And a snowstorm of gulls)

The sea is always in my words
in my aims and in my undertakings
concealed and unsuspected
and like the writing that will not shine through
until the letter is burned to a crisp
Until I am hardened and formed
shaped into a star
into a triumphant arch

A Descendant From Snow

I heard winter bees:
they went woolly, flew from branch to branch, collecting snow.

I heard footsteps:
step by step, generations of withdrawal.

I saw the track:
the monogram of a boot, printed in the snow.

I spelled out:
said a prayer for the missing one.

Troubled, I went out into the whirling snow and shoveled
toward the cry. Enormous lasso loops
swept over the hurricane lamp.

I lay down; dug and dug.
It grew dark. Deep in the avalanche
I lay blind and whimpering.

Gradually it grew light. A pallor
brushes my eyelids. In the sun's sealing-wax
I am sealed up. Growing numb.

I give a start:
then disappear like a stick of kindling wood,
like a cold shot toward the sun.

Appalachian Spring

A tuning fork on the mountain
dancing aerial wires,
paper kites over Maryland . . .
Spring's pilot racing his engines beyond the heights,
and in a small town of German origin
we lingered for a while.
In flowered smocks
stood grayhaired spinsters, breathing,
bewitched between the haystacks
and whispering antennae.
Slowly the valley began to resound.
The sky appeared to be seized by a dream,
and in the fragrance of bonfires and diesel oil
the April twilight's field of images was conjured up.

The Poet in Connecticut
(Wallace Stevens)

Poetry—a blue antenna
strung from coast to coast—
and birds play
amid the trees' telephones.
Humming teleprinter forests . . .
and once in a while,
at the right hour, after five,
after the business day has dropped away,
once in a while
a winged being
(a blackbird?
a seraph with a crown of glazed paper
or halo of wood shavings?)
that sets the wire vibrating,
sets itself down,
tests the intonation—
und macht Musik . . .
From their graves the dead rise,
soldiers in congealed armor,
with spider-web banners
and jasmine wreaths.
He watches them come like America's true sons,
heavy yet tender on the horizon's boards,
bending under the weight of the future . . .
The summer evening is purified, transformed,
and with a gold lining's whisper

Europe peels away, a leaf of tinfoil
from the hundred and fourth floor
and drops into the river.
The heart flutters in the deafening elevator.
His eye closes round a star,
a star, the son of a star . . .

The Scream
(Francis Bacon)

A head slit open by a scream—
a world no greater than the range of the scream.
And there he sits, the dignitary, the pope
or whoever, behind an iron gate
of black brush strokes.
Even the animal has opened itself,
hanging slaughtered in the inscrutable.
Why does a being scream?
For many reasons.
There are those who shake as they scream,
ready to fly off.
Do they wish to fly? And there are those
who grow indistinct behind their cries,
whirling in the vortex of the scream:
their faces thin slowly in space.
Here we see a human being: borne by its scream,
purged by its crying, almost worn out.
What is left may be called peace.

Eurydice Snatched Away

His tears filled with eyes—

When she walked away on the high curved bridge
out into darkness or light,
he watched her garments fold.
Glimpsed her foot, saw its imprint.

And he saw with many eyes
her movement in air, erect
toward the unavoidable
darkness or light,
as she vanished in the vortex
where wind and air
are swept into a spiral:

Where on a whirling staircase
she is swept up and off
          in all her shimmer.

Linnaeus at Work on *Nemesis Divina*

Bent over the notebook—
what bitter ink: and the words
clog in his hand,
only ice plants, the flower of heinous crime!—

The Dutch stove cools down.
His thought glides, once more,
from illness to the Uppsala Garden,
with musicians and laurels . . .

The windowpane rattles
as a cart scrapes over the crusted snow.
An evil omen or a joyous one?—
And a quivering seizes his pen.

"This for son Carl, for his education.
This for the enemies the Lord has removed.
Fortunes, acclamations, decorations
driven up in a snowy cloud,
along with me, a dust mote,
in that steady swirl:
This for the world, which seems to diminish.

His thought darkens, gets lost; he hears the cart
and watches it for a second pass through the groves:
with corybantes and garlands,
the sun, Flora's skirt, a weathervane . . .

But a chariot of ice proceeds toward Hammarbyn.
His hand shrinks, and from the sheet
stares a twisted word: "Stenbrohult."*

Hammarbyn: Linnaeus's summer house outside Uppsala.

Stenbrohult: the town in the province of Smäland where Linnaeus was born in 1707.

Nemesis Divina: book title and Linnaeus's concept.

Master Linnaeus

A bird was in the room; he made comic movements with his
    beak.
The window trembled on its catch, the pen wrote gaily, and
    Phoebus
blew into the writing. The wellsprings of language lay open,
    blue as ink,
there was mirrored Uppsala's Botanical Garden and heaven's
    lovely sunlight,
the bird's feather and the hand guiding the quill.
Now it stayed on its course, and he gazed out the open window:
the bird was gone. Now he felt lonely, a cloud stood in the
    sunlight
and his thought saddened, lingering over Gotland's roses.
And the body sensed, growing farther back through the years,
the post-horse's jerk at a Lapland station.
(It grew cold. Was he already old?)
Then the clock struck in the dome, he gave a start and ended his
    letter
with a twist, ironically, then took up his cloak and left the house.

There lay the green plain bending down with grain, there was
    Master Linnaeus
on a field trip with his court. He slowed down, listened,
raised his finger to worship. Thus one stood still, drinking in
    nature,
imbibing its sweet fragrance, reading its magic patterns.
The master explained; he brought scholars forward in a half-
    circle,

~

opened the flower, pointed at the bee in the flower and the
    beauty of both;
taught their nature and fertilization's secrets, lectured on
everything's ordered form, creation's all-wise structure.
All things had meaning, all was reason and unity, oneness, man
    was part
of a whole that Providence carried and governed. Then he
    stopped.
A snail was seen glistening in the grass; he took it up and smiled
at its simplicity, at its sluggish, benumbed senses.

He stood quietly in the countryside, listened, failing to notice
the singular halo, the bird's ring around his head,
the plant's eyes. There was the bird from his room. A horse
neighed in the distance. The castle stood on the ridge in peace.
Soon the harvests would billow. He recalled the Blue Virgin's
    waves.
Soon his soul would depart. (He thought of the cruel goddess,
Nemesis, but he felt the strength of his innocence.) He cheered
    up,
set off for the city, where the chestnuts' shadows lay heavy.
The bird perched again on his windowsill.

Spring's Volte-Face

The sun porch shakes
when the light strikes
and the concertina of spring heat
gradually begins to limber up.
Houses rouse themselves, roofs boom,
and in the drain pipes the sheet metal resounds,
zinc-blue,
musically, with the craft of the artisan.

The Song of the Tree

During the final approach before landing, a tree looms forth for a few seconds.

It stands before a clump of other trees in a field. Impossible to make it out clearly from this altitude, amid the air buffeting below the fusilage. Just an ordinary tree, drawing nourishment from a subterranean vein of water, lapping up the reluctant drops from a drying rill. The leaves probably brown in the quivering heat, congealed into copper in the early afternoon sun, where the shadows begin to ooze forth from the forms of things.

Obsession in the observer in the vibrating craft, while it descends over a highway and a field, where a flock of jackdaws or rooks are flung to the side like the flakes over a sooty fire. The ground trembles under the light metal, it burns maize-yellow even toward the horizon, but he fixes his glance on the tree. He thinks, while the plane banks yet another time and all air appears to be thrown backwards, that some day he must return to this tree on the outskirts of this village, a house not so far from the tree, with chickens and ducks coming into view down there in a dazzling second and the tree's song about something that is not to be found anywhere else.

Not so that everything would be otherwise, if he were to return to this point, the lonely tree in the alien land. That loneliness would cease there and a vein of water would burst forth. Only therewith a divination, a jolt, which transmits itself through his body, of a return to an existence that had long ago passed into oblivion.

Lars Lundkvist
(1928–   )

Lars Lundkvist, born in Umeå, province of Västerbotten, northern Sweden, received his certificate as a secondary school teacher in 1954 and later studied at the University of Uppsala. When he made his debut with *Offertrumma* (Sacrificial drum, 1950), he struck a new chord in Swedish poetry by employing incantations, troll formulas, and rigmaroles from the mythology of the Swedish Saami minority.

In his attempt to incorporate ritualistic elements in his art he managed to create connections between images that are as abrupt as they are effective. "Only the *nåjd*, only the possessed conjurer" is capable of discovering the underlying meaning of reality, he suggested. His subsequent collections of poetry are applications of this suggestion, especially *Njaka* (Njaka, 1953), *Nåjd* (Shaman, 1961) and *Blå Berg Och Vit Sol* (Blue mountains and white sun, 1964). In *Bilder i en Silversked* (Images in a silver spoon, 1969) he widened his scope, although much of the same magic is present. But in the collection *Förvåna mig* (Make me astonished, 1974) he turns to scenes and themes other than those of Lapland: love, everyday life, episodes and memories from the poet's childhood, and of his later life, predominate.

In later collections the magic elements are more concerned with real or surreal events primarily in the far north. "He now peoples his poems with retired school teachers, surveyors, bus drivers, herring fishermen, reading clinics, seamstresses, old age homes, carpenters and planters. But as in the early books the central theme is the precariousness of human life," Olle Carlsson wrote.

Lundkvist later becomes an interpreter of suffering. It is as if Freud were speaking: "There are too many dead people, too much suffering in this world."

Lars Lundkvist's way through incantation toward "a wilder will to believe in God" (Staffan Söderblom) is reflected in the following prayer, "an appalling prayer, the most egotistical prayer there is" according to the poet:

LET ME LIVE LONG

HEALTHY AND STRONG

IN BODY AND SOUL

TO THE DELIGHT OF SOMEONE

CURIOUS

AMEN

The poet Staffan Larsson has pointed out some of Lars Lundkvist's influences. Among them are Bo Setterlind, Helmer Grundström, and Federico García Lorca: "*Nåjd* is Lars Lundkvist's attempt to create a Swedish counterpart to Ezra Pound's *Cantos*. In *Bilder i en silversked* (Images in a silver spoon) references are made to Goethe, Dante, Dostoevsky, and, later on, to St. John Perse, Neruda, Lorca, and, finally, to the surrealists. In all his writings the Bible plays a predominant part.

The Nordic Council (Copenhagen) awarded Lars Lundkvist the Grand Prize for poetry in 1991. The selections included here are taken from *Korn* (Grain, 1983) and the prize-winning *Tjuka* (Growth on a tree, 1991). These are the first of his poems to be translated into English.

Niobe

Niobe
was changed into stone.

She was proud of her twelve children,
not grateful for them.

Arrows
pierced her heart.

gray lichen
now grows on her stone.

Fire and sulfur!
The archeologists drink wine at the inn

and spice their food
with oregano.

Niobe and Mephisto cry out their anguish
in supplication.

—How do you read?
—The way the Devil reads the Bible, said the Devil.

He Caught a Ptarmigan

He caught a ptarmigan
early one morning.

When he had eaten it,
he wept in gratitude

for the gift
of having been allowed to eat his fill.

From his tears
lilacs sprang.

Lilacs do not grow on the mountain,
but even today miracles can occur.

Escaping

He was the only one who succeeded in escaping,
all the others sank into the sea.

On the island of Svartholmen he drank water
from a cold spring.

There he died
with his hands clasped in prayer.

The mites did not understand this sign
of gratitude.

but the strangers, who buried him
realized the blessing of the water.

On the stone they marked the water level
and his name. It was Moses.

Two Lives
For David Wagoner

I remember him,
the boy who became a salmon

and was killed by his father
in confusion and ignorance.

When the father saw his blood
he dug a pit

and lay down in it
without Bible or hymn book, without faith.

The fishing line and the fishing knife
he swallowed.

The date of this occurrence
cannot be determined.

Companions

The street sweeper and the redstart both know
much about old boots and plant lice.

They keep quiet and at dusk drink
a glass of beer at the Seven Anchors.

Before the chairs are turned over
and the bats arrive,

the redstart sings of the Congo,
of those who have drowned in Africa

or have succumbed
to drought or hunger.

—Look at my wing, she says.
It has a bullet hole.

Do you wish to shoot me?
Shoot now, the moon is on the wane.

—Hell, no says the street sweeper.
Now I shall play my accordion.

An ornithologist
saw them both fly off toward the southwest.

Uncertainty

The woman wears a shawl
with a copper clip.

When she sinks down through the earth
a spring wells forth.

The trees around them dropped
their fruit and leaves,

which are watered by the wild animals of the forest
and are guarded by a gray hen.

The singers
are hidden in the greenery.

Don't ask me about the meaning of all this.
Ask the Almighty.

Fate

—What time is it?
asked the Dalecarlian* when the horse died.

The clock was wrong,
it hadn't been wound for a year.

The Dalecarlian admitted his negligence
and shot himself behind the outdoor privy.

Insects, having come from far away,
wanted to tell of the Devil's land,

but it was too late.
That's why they gobbled him up.

—————

*An inhabitant of the Swedish province of Dalecarlia.

Examination I

I saw her
between blue mussels and algae.

She was dead then.
She had a summa cum laude in Greek and Latin.

I saw her in a knife with her father's eyes
and her mother's smile.

The late-come child
had become a blasphemy, a taunt.

Hops can grow along the wall of a house
without strings

and nettles thrive
in hail and rain.

How can a withered tulip
be pruned and fertilized?

This is an evil tale,
an unreality with the scent of a camellia.

Congratulation

Today I saw an angel—
a ten-year-old girl,

the child
I had always wished for.

I wanted to hug her
but her mother's umbrella was sharp.

Might I send her a violet
or a radio antenna as forgiveness?

Protect her, God,
make her into the Virgin Mary's successor.

An angel—
I saw heaven in her eyes.

Transformations

She put on a green skirt
and flew away in a cloud across southern Sweden.

Her intention was unclear.
Was she looking for her lover,

a pastry-cook or a county police commissioner,
the county council's director of invalids

or a grocer?
Her purpose was unclear.

After a prelude by willow warblers and herring gulls
she sang above southern Podunk and Hackensack.

Now she is seen sometimes
as a cadaver with green claws.

To some
she is an osprey with a herring in her beak,

to others
a child who died on delivery.

Summer

The lupine are blooming
and the cabbage is yellow.

God is on vacation and the philosophers are asleep.
Saint Peter is fishing for whitefish.

In your hair mignonette and milkwort bloom,
a fragrance of linen and newly baked unleavened bread.

We live in a time without limitation
between two large waterfalls.

in a belief
that condemnation is impermanent.

The roe-deer
is not frightened by our presence.

At night
with its muzzle it caresses our cheeks.

Faith

A bird
is perched on the roof.

From there it sees our window
and our love,

the orchids and the teddy bear
who converses with a girl.

The bird is condemned to death,
that the bureaucrats have decided.

But the bird has laid an egg,
its hiding place is secret.

She is not afraid,
she feels secure.

"We shall return!"

Knowledge, devotion, and pangs of conscience
can often be united.

Examination II

The door opens—
the girls run out of the music school,

out into the sun,
to the grass, roses, and jasmine.

Who asks for a six horsepower locomobile
or a tortoise with 40,000 testicles?

Who mourns Anacreon's death in Sierra Leone
and the dead bumblebee on the porch?

And who is the man in Joensuu
who carries around a man's skull in a jar of alcohol?

Before them
a clarinet concert of Mozart!

And there are the funny ladies
who feed pigeons! And there is the ox on the roof!

Delilah furtively shaves off Samson's hair
and across the fjord run little old ladies,

their skirts over their heads,
to steal butter on Flisön.

Still the world is changeable—
a foetus weighs less than a grape.

It is a long way to the H minor Mass of Bach,
a long way to the *Stabat Mater* and to Death.

Visit

Before he came home from America,
for the first time in forty years
he wrote a letter: "Make burbot soup, Vanja!"

Then he went to the England skerry,
the old wharf where his father
had worked. He dug in the earth

and found rivets and bolts from
Johannisfors and remnants of cross-bars
and ribs from the sloop Lovisa. He wept

The arctic raspberry ditch had grown together,
the fence wood had rotted, the harrow was scrap.
But the store on the mountain was still there:

3 PINE CONES FOR A PIECE OF RAG
2 STONES FOR A PIECE OF TINTED GLASS.
5 HERRING EYES FOR A CUP OF LEMONADE.

And what joy it is to be able to buy a hunk
of sugar for a shirt button!
Or an old key for a crow's feather!

Our Father, he thought, and placed
a dollar bill beneath a triangular stone.
*Is that all there is?**

One month later came a letter, the last,
with a postcard, from Seattle:
"Thanks for the burbot soup, Vanja!"

————————

*In English in the original.

The Way It Is

At all times, in all parts of the world
thousands of poems have been written about a woman's lap—

on slates and on parchment, in caves,
in sewers, in fat books and on trees,

on urinals and outhouses,
walls and ceilings, on cement and on newly fallen snow:

a water hole for the tiger to rest by,
a well where the antelope can slake his thirst.

a red sun,
an amaryllis and an iron foundry,

a cold spring in the forest for the hare and the fox,
a steam engine, a sparrow in the willow, a slaughterhouse.

And the woman's thighs: two wandering trees
with grown-together crowns, two kids from Livorno

seeking their father, two windmills, two rollers
in a printing press. Lunar eclipse! Mystery!

Incompatible and indifferent similes
for the tired one,

antiquated humiliating wordplay
for the feeble and the sick.

But for the child, the youth and the woman herself!
And for the lovesick one, the one overcome by lust.

Merciless

I am so happy today,
    enveloped in a divinity
that someone
wishes me to discover.

I could
    run to Scehensaschan in the Sahara
or up to Akantjakk
and roll down like a black pudding into the lake.

I could
    rummage about in the Swedish alphabet
and delete many figures
in birth certificates and old annals

and throw a steamroller thirty feet
    in the air and devour
small packets of needles and nails or
a small tractor. So happy am I.

Around me: those who are dying,
    far away and close by.
Some of my friends have had their legs amputated
and steel balls inserted into their bodies,

nerves atrophied and eyes dimmed
    and a poison cupboard in their souls.

When they take a spill on the kitchen floor
amid their crutches and wheelchairs

they see Death very clearly.
    One of them says:
    —How many centimeters will they
cut off on Tuesday? My second leg.

But I am well: I live in peace
    and feel that I am loved.
My kidneys function properly
and my lungs and heart muscles and the little pineal gland.

And my memory is good. I know that the battle
    at Narva took place in the year 1700,
that the peace at Knäred was concluded in 1613
and that the liquor ration book was discontinued in 1955.

And I can communicate with animals:
    I am not as wise as St. Francis
but just now when the cock crowed
I spoke to an October fly.

When I let it out through the window
    it blinked at me.
But that fly was mischievous.
It was not at me that it blinked

but at my beloved
who just then took off
her saffron dressing-gown.

Good gracious! She is standing there naked.

The Stone

Put your head here and rest for a while. But do not fold back the moss and the lichen—I am cold now, it is October and we expect snow, I and my friends, the springtails and the rotifers, the pine-wing and the other inhabitants of the cosmos, snails, larvae, mushrooms, mites, and roundworms. Rest a while by an old man who will outlive you and your children, and all beings on this earth. Decades and centuries—seconds in my tabulator.

Here I have lain since the Ice Age, the time prior to that I've forgotten. Many of my relatives possess knowledge about the entire earth and its history and know the names of all the Kings, Emperors, and Despots, all the Revolutionaries and Executioners, Peasant Leaders, Warriors, and Tyrants, the names of all the plants and animals. But I am still so young.

Am I ugly? I have nonetheless been admired for my form and my colors and been painted by a woman artist. Many have also peacefully leaned against me for a while in the sun, and the day before yesterday a few minutes before the rain came intercourse was consummated here among the twigs, among newts and spiders. *Caelestis felicitas*!

Many call me dumb and dangerous, a friend of supernatural elements: imps and evil-minded pixies, evil goblins and pregnant wood spirits. The badgers spread rumors!

I am only a stone in the forest that feels the rotation of the seasons and the eclipses of the planets, a stone that needs neither a divining rod, perch scales, nor plummet to predict frost and precipitation, thunder, or misfortune. I trust the clouds, the wind, and the sun. It hurts sometimes when the frost is hard and the lodestone turns at two p.m. on a summer day.

~

Did you see it? The lightning flash in the spruce tree, in the squirrel's eye? Did you hear it? The goshawk's wing beats and the mouse's screams? Do you feel the fragrance of wild rosemary and the leaves and the elk calf's droppings, a sense of the ineffable, the unarticulated? And listen—to the bells in your inner ear, to the beating of our heart!

You want me to tell you about history's lies and the border between love and compassion, which is difficult to experience and comprehend, about Good and Evil. No, I have seen too many corpses and know that man is not now wiser than he was in the time of Abraham. I keep silent.

Now return to your home. Soon the sun will set behind the paper mill and flash in the hospital windows, the evening coils of smoke already rise from the river. Go home to the things that are close to you, play a waltz by Chopin and contemplate an old picture or an engraving from India or a chair. Someone is waiting at the door.

Does she love you?

The Pin

On a hill outside the city
stands an oak tree three fathoms high

In the shade of this tree
a woman once sat waiting.

She combed her hair
and hid a pin in the bark

When the man came and lay down in the grass
with his head in her lap

It was then five P.M.

When he opened his eyes
he saw her face—

a medallion
in the tree's huge crown!

A gem, a sapphire
enveloped by wild bees!

Or did he then see the melancholy,
the wrinkles around her eyes,

the wrinkles of the neck
and the lines of weariness around her mouth?

A tree
and a pin in the bark of the tree.

The birds also are dead.

Observation

The shadows of the trees—
    more precious every day,
irreplaceable
    like childhood memories
and dead cells.

What trees? Elm or linden,
    ash or maple?
Trees think in different ways
    and speak in different tongues
at different points of time—

you cannot interpret their shadows
    by means of the height of the sun,
the species of tree
    and its approximate age.
The shadows are in your soul.

The shadows of pebbles—
    they, too, are ever more precious
each day. Their wisdom
    is older than that of the trees,
primeval, unfathomable.

Young Love

Our ancestors remain silent,
classical antiquity, the entire world history—

no one denies us the happiness
to love just now.

—At the *open* fire?
On the old carpet from Hamadan?

Certainly the birch logs do not betray us
and the poker is my friend.

I have also talked to the telephone
and spoken with the jackdaws at seven this evening,

these jackdaws, these restless jackdaws,
the consolation of the fool, God's messengers.

And Uncle Alexander in his silver frame,
he who danced the *trepak* in 1858

at the Big Market in St. Petersburg
with a glass of champagne on his head

and a rose in his hand, says:
—Surely you have read the Books of Psalms?

But my horn shalt thou exalt
  like the horn of a unicorn:
Thou shall be anointed with fresh oil.

The geezer is crafty—
he has changed a word or two in the text!

Early

DA MI BASIA MILLE
DEINDE CENTUM

It is seven
and this is the first day:

But the sun is so strong—
I pull the curtain,

the blue curtain with fish,
jelly-fish and starfish on it,

DEIN MILLE ALTERA,
DEIN SECUNDA CENTUM

But the birds, the great tit,
the marsh tit, the sparrows, and the magpie,

and all the fruit trees in bloom,
apple and cherry, plum and pear?

I shall play *"Et expecto
resurrectionum mortuorum"*

and frighten away all the birds
and fetch a saw

and a crowbar
and a yellow power shovel.

Beloved, now we shall celebrate
with a real feast!

We invite them all,
the birds, the trees, and the sun.

DEINDE USQUE ALTERA MILLE,
DEINDE CENTUM.

It is a long way to the Serpent-carrier,
and the difference is great

between seven o'clock in spring
and seven in autumn.

And joy is never improper
if it is genuine, as in a child.

And this is the first day.
Send your bread across the water!

Kerstin Thorék
(*1934–*)

Kerstin Thorék grew up in the coastal city of Skellefteå in northern Sweden. She went through business school on the advice of her parents, but very reluctantly. At the age of nineteen, she left for Stockholm, where she worked in an office, a bookstore, a news agency, the National Bacteriological Laboratory, and a film company while she pursued her theater studies. Through adult education classes she eventually acquired an academic degree. She was active in student theater and produced plays by Vladimir Mayakovsky and Sonja Åkesson. Her production of the Åkesson play received first prize at the student theater festival in Zagreb. In the spring of 1964 her first book *Ta ner änglarna* (Bring down the angels) appeared. There followed *Skärmaskinen* (The cutting machine, 1966), *I stället för album* (Instead of an album, 1977), *Anatomiska sånger* (Anatomical songs, 1980). As the latter title indicates, Thorék here deals quite a bit with her own body, its anatomy and physiology. There is irony in many of the poems, as in the almost parodic lines:

> In my saffron yellow dress
> I become excited,
> as good as nougat.

One of the best poems has a different kind of sensitivity:

Too late for cat's foot
Already July and I pick
lyme grass instead

On my way back home by the forest path
a paralyzed, chewing hare
frozen fast against a granite boulder
hoping that he too
will be taken for a block of stone

As long as possible he wishes to believe
that I shall believe in this art of illusion

Even I remain still
sense the animal's rising adrenalin
Finally neither of us can stand it any longer
I cleave fear into two dripping halves of fruit
the saliva wets simultaneously our dry palates
And suddenly the hairy reflex is dissolved

in the moss.

Thorék's other titles are: *Öppna tal* (Open speeches, 1983), *Från Härs och Tvärs till Blåbärsvers. Barnbok.* (From hither to thither to blueberry—verse, 1983), *Glädjens fragment* (The fragments of joy, 1984).

She has translated the Romanian poet Gabriela Melinescu's *Kyskhetslöftet* (The vow of chastity), with Ingrid Duke and M. Ljungberg, 1975, and Eeva Kilpi, the Finnish poet, *Sånger om kär-lek* (Songs of love, with Ulla-Mari Kankaanpää and Kerstin Lindqvist, 1980).

Thorék grew up in a generous, loving environment as an only child and "with great faith in life," as she said in an interview. While her orientation is toward Eastern literatures, she said she read Eliot's poems when she was fourteen and Eliot received the Nobel Prize for Literature. She has always been a movie and theatre buff and feels she has learned from the montage technique of films, especially the films of Tarkovsky.

Thorék has long been attracted to Caravaggio's art: the coarseness, brutality, in combination with the metaphysical quality, the ecstatic side by side with the down-to-earth and the repulsive. And the composition, the dramatic structure of the images clearly appeals to her.

Several years ago Thorék saw Caravaggio's *Medusa* in the Uffizi in Florence for the first time, and "suddenly it struck me: he has painted himself: His insatiable sorrow changed into rage."

Travel is important to Thorék, especially the encounter with foreign cultures. In the early 1980s she spent a month in Peru. This visit was the basis of the "Quipous Suite," parts of which are included here. Vallejo, Marina Tsvetaeva, Emily Dickinson, Wislawa Szymborska, and, of course, Tomas Tranströmer, are sources of inspiration for her.

A recurring theme in her poetry is the cosmic perspective. One of her *Anatomical Songs* has as an epigraph the following passage from Sara Lidman: "The cosmic element in man is the prime mover of everything, of rebellion, and must not be neglected. If man is a robot, liberation has no meaning." *Anatomical Songs* has a strong ecological aspect, emphasizing the connection between humankind, animal, and nature. The book was written before Chernobyl and deals with the world after it.

Caravaggio's Knife

I

In the cathedral of knives the ringing of bells
widens the cracks in the cast iron
and the crevice in the breastbone

All the soul's voices rain down
Few dare come hither at night
and yet there is this thronging of the absolute
Only in an embrace does the knife lose its sharp edge

II

I, Michelangelo Merisi, born at Caravaggio
in 1573. Origin and destination: background of poverty.

From the beginning endowed with the genius of my eyes
and the lightning of my thought. I, Michelangelo Merisi, the Master
and Painter of the tormented dark recesses,
the bodies of the desired ones, the secret, fugitive hiding places.

In this century art was intended only to adorn
the halls of churches and princes but my Matthew
in *Matthew and the Angel*
is a pickpocket from the area.
Indeed, all my disciples—a Peter or a Paul—
                    I took from the streets.
And who can forget the young male Tuscan prostitute

I picked up because of his bushy eyebrows?
In my work even pimps are canonized.

My house is a house in rage
my knife is a knife in an embrace
My desire is centered in my small intestine
my insults are best suited
                    to the slop-pail

From pub to pub along the dock
and yet I shun the crowd.
Crouching, I paint the elemental,
the emotional remnants, the sinews,
the revolting physiognomies.

The painting called *The Conversion of St. Paul*
peopled by pigments of lampblack and bone black
The man on the ground with his legs spread apart
below the horse's cautious hooves.
Violence was never so serene as in his flesh

They whisper: "He blasphemes."
But I, Caravaggio, know
that the light must rise from the forsaken
must ooze from the cold sack of being

They assume that I never painted any self-portrait.
But fired by my own rage I painted *The Medusa*.

and I painted myself as that fury on the convex
rounded shield. My severed head with the dark halo
of writhing bronze serpents, I stare at you across the centuries

Marina Tsvetaeva

I the one thirsting for purification always on the point
of biting through all reality's seal
Not dreamlike but like reality
I make my way through the ravagings of the granite nights
Change quite unexpectedly, abruptly, out of my blue guise
and am transformed into my own scheming dynamiter
Libidinously I explode the domains of
lead-heavy thought and inhibition
and space fills cautiously with my words
whirled down, concentrated and excavated
Thus chaos pulls the carpet off the stairs
and groping and stumbling
but never taciturn I plunge right down
into reality that has been split open
escorted by a feather-adorned, painted shaman
myself
The whitened sorrow that has hit me
has picked the shell from the moist egg
the down and
the brittle bones from the bird body
But still there is something that lifts from the ground
The opened top of a grand piano
A black wing, immense, in its attempts
to cleave this oceanic, painful surge.

Contradictions

This is the way I want the world to look on a day off
when work has given up its attempt
to race against itself and ambition
is shut down like a windswept post office
in some distant land.
No messages are received or answered.
It is only consciousness that methodically
without stopping fills its presence to the brim.
It is like a refreshing wine barrel into which
now and then I sybaritically dip my tongue.
Yes, consciousness is indeed a white burgundy matured
in the dim gulf between two kinds of clanging sound: feeling
and intellect. (The voices before and after the great Event.)

Considerably later, toward midnight, something
gains in strength and threatens to crowd me out
onto the street. Feverishly I search
for a connection but the only thing that comes
to me is this: ". . . I contradict myself as you yourself do."

Trying to enclose
the entire width and depth
of one's conscience
is like catching
Saturn in a butterfly net.

The Andes

From the section Quipous; *a quipous is a knotted string,*
the knots representing different numbers,
used by the Incas to send or record numerical data.

4.
The mountains rise higher than the castle of the condors
The black mountains are asleep above the cloud formations—
a metallic, tertiary sleep.
In their hidden grottos linger
the souls of the betrayed
the anguish has colored the stone walls
lean as silk through the millennia
Deep below the ground
the bedrock also is asleep
even down to its roots it sleeps
with the exploitation erased, flown
into a mantle

In the Andes the earth has gathered a strength
as great as God's wrath
rich in selenium and metaphysical as myth itself
as old as the birth of continents
as compact as the collected weight of matter
The folded mountains sleep
What will make the range burst some day?

5.

By the bald market square
in Concepción we get off;
a cracked, leaning chapel incessantly
screwing up its eyes toward the north
as if there were something there to discover, perhaps a lake
The air is slow jelly
nothing moves,
the fans of cool air are guarded
out of sight

As if drawn by a dull magnet
we head toward the middle of the square
toward the introspective fountain
that in vain hallucinates about water
water, freckled with rust,
water, earth-umber like *chicha* and coca
water like holy water
water like salt sea and urine

On the side of the shadows
the Indian women crouched among tin cans,
dogs and children
Their elegant white hats stand
like puff-balls emerging from the cracked earth
There is a foreboding
of some other mystical world that eludes me
however long I stay here
The heat lingers
soiled above the square
in its own tyranny

carefully embalming the thin
burned-out foliage
Existence breathes patience
and I receive it

With a calm as wide open
as a Titicaca gap
deep down in the dry depth
mysteriously something beats violently
But you do not hear it.

6. LIMA

An energetically crowing cock in the midst of this
town of millions makes me wake up too early,
sticky from the moist heat. Somebody has called Lima
the heaven of women, men's purgatory, and donkeys' hell.
Thus I awakened in heaven.
The others have gone and I am left by myself. But
that was the way I wanted it. According to Stendhal, Lima
is a mysterious, impassioned city with
"a loneliness created for the souls who love
Petrarch's sonnets and Mozart's music." Loneliness
which is my passion.

7.

In a few hours the fragrance from bakeries
and bars will reach me; I shall go out and search for
the first university on the continent (while the others
search for their livelihood), I shall increase my
feeling for the world, I shall write poetry at a

café near Jiron de la Union while an old
man with a broken violin plays out of tune, I shall . . .
But now a music reaches me which can only be heard
during intense anxiety. A requiem. *Rex tremendae*.
I balance my loneliness on my shoulders.

8.

There was no freedom but only security for society.
Not everything was perfect in the paradise of the Incas.
—Ernesto Cardenal

During the night's unsteady
virtuously acrobatic bus ride
in Huascarán's massif
she awakens with a start
Catches sight of a window on the mountain
It is open
It calls for something
for someone who has traveled long
for five hundred years.

9.

In the low houses
the kerosene lamps flicker when the farm woman
steps in through the low door
She carries a wind egg in her rough hand
in its place a star
has come loose
She holds forth the wind egg
What will she get for it

at the market? Nothing. Nothing.
But darkness embraces us and through its mottled texture
we make out the contours of a nest. Then we see
that the world is without a shell. Unprotected.

The heat presses its hot lid
over the landscape.
The field mice wink
The serpent unrolls its full power
on the granite rock.

Close to a high-power line two
drowsy runners are resting
before
before it happens;
in a while the landscape's center of gravity
will move outside the landscape
as if to prevent an imbalance
in the stratosphere.
It turns over. Gravel begins to move.
Gravely the two men turn around.

Epigram

Still your impressions
in my innermost labyrinths
your ball of yarn still winding
in my soul's labyrinth
What robust myths
we must once have created!

But against our shadows,
mutual Minotaurs
we were both defeated

KERSTIN THORÉK

The Airstrip

On a clear newly-scoured fall evening I tend to
my slow dog out on the open field
and I think that the field
is a dark-green, shiny moist runway
on which waiting has been packed together
as the land ice once was packed
beyond the limits of its capacity;
an attention of the ground compressed
into vague wave movements in the wet grass
where I walk with my dawdling dog
and the dog suddenly hears something
that I don't hear.
He stops suddenly (as only he can)
and presses his ears attentively backward.
What is it?
A cosmic jingling shattering the stratosphere
or only an earthworm that happens to turn
over in the slippery grass?

So the dog hears what I cannot hear
and earthworms can be cut in two
and yet start out again in their two halves.

But are we the only ones who can join together
cosmos, dog, and earthworm
in a trinity?
In order later, much later, and in a wider

perspective, we shall be able to tear
the riddle's ancient woven wrapping and then
without forewarning like a "lightning from a clear sky"
be able to find our way into relationships
where the still-healed nature constantly broods.

KERSTIN THORÉK

Anatomical Song

I can't be had in furnished rooms,
you say
Put me into an unfurnished one then!
Cosier than this
it's never going to be
however much furniture we drag together here

Reality can't allow itself to be disguised
Outside it is incessantly broken apart
crunch after crunch.
like your sweet Rye-King sandwiches
The entrails well forth in the sticky honey.
the alphabet
open in every direction
like continent after continent
word witness after word witness
down to lost time
when letter upon letter
were literally nailed into metal and stone

Can you in the shiny crucible of the computer
gather up the thinking elements
that move even in the chaos of the human galaxy?

Toward the East we outline Alpha
toward the West, an Omega
By manipulating them we touch
part of the whole and control ourselves
even though our tongues are on the edge of convulsion.

Lars Gustafsson
(1936–)

Lars Gustafsson was born in the city of Västerås, capital of Västmanland province, east central Sweden, where he also went to school. He entered the University of Uppsala, where he received his Fil. lic. (Ph.D.) in 1961 and his Fil. Dr. (in philosophy) in 1979. He served as editor of *Bonniers Litterära Magasin*, 1960–72, as literary critic of the liberal *Expressen*, 1961–80, and as critic on the conservative *Svenska Dagbladet* since 1981. He has been a member of the International Petrarca Prize Committee since 1979 and a corresponding member, Akademie der Wissenschaften und der Literatur Mainz, since 1971, and a member, Akademie der Künste, Berlin, since 1973. An adjunct professor at the University of Texas, Austin, he has received numerous prizes, including the Henrik Steffen Prize, Hamburg, 1985.

If Lars Gustafsson has a long life and produces twenty or so plays, he will easily surpass Strindberg's life achievement: fifty-five volumes of prose, plays, essays, and poetry. At the latest count (1990), Gustafsson (then fifty-four) had fifty-five books to his credit. Several of them have been translated into German and from German into Hebrew and Arabic. Three volumes of poetry are available in English: *Lars Gustafsson: Selected Poems*, translated by Robin Fulton, New Rivers Press, 1972); *Warm Rooms and Cold*, translated by Yvonne L. Sandstroem, Copper Beach Press, 1975); and *The Stillness of the World Before Bach*, translated by Robin

Fulton, Philip Martin, Yvonne L. Sandstroem, Harriett Watts, and Christopher Middleton, New Directions, 1988.

On a summer day in 1950, when Lars Gustafsson, at the age of fourteen, was out with his parents on an excursion on a narrow spit of land extending into a lake in North Västmanland, he received a call to write poetry. "A dipper hung over the water out there, the evening breeze came in a rush, the dark stream kept flowing in its quiet inexorable rhythm." When he left the spot, he knew that he was given over to poetry, and "that that language, which in some mysterious way was identical with the wordless authority of the scenery, from then on was my language." That the call to poetry was exceptionally strong is shown by the fact that he wrote hundreds of poems in the next few years.

In the course of writing poetry for more than forty years, Lars Gustafsson has moved from rather long poems in the 1960s (in the Eliot vein) to ballads, sonnets, and didactic poems in the 1970s, and now he employs the montage technique of films to his advantage for his own blend of pensive lyric.

An ethnographic, philosophical, or historical interest informs much of Gustafsson's poetry, which, in many ways, is both unromantic and strange. His artistically most successful and effective analyses of the human predicament to date are 1) *Artesiska brunnar cartesianska drömmar* (Artesian wells cartesian dreams, 1980) which takes off from Descartes's statement that "waking life and dream never can be kept apart by reliable criteria." "How can one then know that waking life is real?" is the question; and 2) *Kärleksförklaring till en sefardisk dam* (Declaration of love to a Sephardic lady, 1970), in which "he weaves together anima myth, political reflections from contemporary times, critical comments on our civilization and what he has seen himself against a backdrop through which the golden yellow light of childhood shines." It is a loose form, but one that makes for very imaginative poetry.

Processes of time, such as transformations or changes in identity, interest Lars Gustafsson greatly, as can be seen repeatedly in the following selections, such as the "Elegy for the Old Mexican Woman and Her Dead Child." In the mirror he catches a glimpse of "this eccentric old man/who is slowly about to/make his way out of my face." When he asks: "How can so many men live in the same body?" the question is related to a problem already considered by ancient Indian philosophers, i.e., the so-called chain of causation. But Lars Gustafsson's time is tied to other concepts, such as imprisonment. Things, for instance, become liberated "when they are let loose again for good/from the domain/of the human, from designs and words and actions."

Lars Gustafsson is in the habit of weaving into his text the multiple problems he sees in language as well. Two of his key symbols call for closer scrutiny: the maze and the well, both suggesting variants of the same problem, that once you are in them, your opportunity to view yourself from the outside ceases.

The machine as a symbol also has deep significance in Gustafsson's poetry. On the subject Yvonne L. Sandstroem has written an enlightening study (*Scandinavian Studies*, vol. 44, No.2, 1972).

Elegy for the Old Mexican Woman
and Her Dead Child

Am I mistaken—
or is the air thinner up here?

In such rarefied air could a swallow
find support for its wing?

Now from the bathroom mirror
looms this eccentric old man

who is slowly making his way
out of my face:

strong, tanned, furrowed,
with blue eyes growing ever colder,

the last of the men I shall be—
not yet entirely formed, but already hinted at.

I try to remember the child who once occupied
the same place in the mirror,

blond, round-cheeked, contented,
resting on little chubby elbows.

How can so many men
live in the same body?

An old woman in Mexico, the paper reports,
was admitted to a hospital for stomach trouble.

An examination revealed that the eighty-six-year-old woman
had for more than sixty years carried a foetus

weighing nine hundred grams; this stone child, a lithopedion,
had accompanied her throughout life.

One might say that she was at once birthplace
and grave for one and the same child.

Graves—those cavities, urns, vaults,
marble crypts or simple holes in the ground—

which we have had with us for thousands of years,
are naturally all a kind of mother.

We try in vain to bring back
the dead to the point of departure.

The Mexican woman was, in her way,
the *ideal grave*. And her child's,

an exemplary life? Mockingbird, what do you want?
You have so many voices, and I don't know

which of them to take seriously,
the scornful one at times, the complaining one at others,

and then, on certain days in early spring,
when moisture still clings to the moss on the oak tree

there is a kind of chortling sound
as if you couldn't quite come out with it properly.

Mockingbird perched in the green oak tree,
what secret are you trying to swallow?

I, too, am an old Mexican woman.
I, too, carry a dead child within me,

but my child is peculiar: it can talk,
it actually keeps talking all the time,

prattling unclearly like all children
who haven't learned to talk; it is not easy

to discover what it wants, but it does want something.
I am not unreasonable: on the contrary,

I know that I stand in a father's place,
trying hard to understand what this child

wants from its life, which is its death.
But it is not easy. It is so unlike me.

And of this world knows nothing.

LARS GUSTAFSSON

Letter to a Tyrant

The long night now recedes.
And what it hid is better seen;

And it is not at all attractive.
It is charnel houses, graves, the dispersed and unaccounted for.

You are very old now, it seems
that Your vision has greatly deteriorated

while others have regained their vision.

Or is it simply that Your horsemen,
Your carrier pigeons, Your once rapid ships

move to an entirely different tempo now?
Exhausted, asthmatic horses, ragged, sickly pigeons

and ships with leaky decks
and poor rotting cordage. They turn up

ever more rarely and often with bad news.
The letters from the fringes of the Empire are few and far
      between.

Are they still there, the "fringes of the Empire"?
Crumbling walls. Plowmen around deserted border forts.

Do they not fear You any longer? Or
is it merely that the "fringes of the Empire"

nowadays run also like knife-sharp lines
through Your own tired old soul? You would sleep now,

if there were a chance to sleep. You would forget
if there were a chance to forget.

And we would gladly put you out of our minds. The pious one
who lost all his sons and wives,

got new wives, new cattle, new sons.
So justice was finally restored,

the disturbed relations were repaired.
And Job died, old in years, as is said.

But who will take on the first sons,
the first wives, the first dead lambs?

Who pleads their cause among the dead?
When You are no longer there to hate?

Ballad on the Paths in Västmanland

Under the visible script of small roads,
dirt roads, farm roads, often with a comb
of grass in the middle between deep wheel tracks,
hidden under the clear-cut area's piles of twigs,
still distinct in the parched moss—
beneath them runs another script: the old paths.
They run from lake to lake, from valley
to valley. They sometimes get deeper,
become very clear, and large bridges
of stone from medieval quarries carry them over black brooks,
at times they vanish over bare ledges,
you easily lose them in marshes, so
imperceptible are they that one moment they are there,
the next they are not. But they keep on,
they always keep on, as long as
you watch for them, these paths persist.
They know what they want and with know-how
they combine a considerable craftiness.
You walk toward the east, the compass constantly points to the east;
in a straight line the path faithfully follows the compass;
all is in order, then suddenly the path veers to the north.
To the north there is nothing. What does the path now want?
Soon a gigantic bog appears,and the path knew it.
It swings around, with the sense of security of one
who has seen things before. It knows where the bog is,
it knows where the mountain becomes too steep, it knows
what happens to those who walk north instead of south
of the lake. It has done all these things

so many times before. That's the entire meaning
of being a path. That it has been done
before. Who made the path? Charcoal burners, fishermen,
bony-armed women collecting wood?
Outlaws, gray and shy like the moss,
still dreaming with the blood of fratricide
on their hands? Autumnal hunters in the tracks
of their faithful harriers with frost-clear bark?
All and none. We make it together,
you too create it on a blustery day when
it is early or late on this earth:
we write out the paths, and the paths remain,
and the paths are smarter than we are,
and know all that we wanted to know.

The Balloonists

See the tall man there in the top hat.
He leans out and reconnoiters toward the west.
It is early, before noon, with light reverberating.

In the distance the city marks time with its bells,
blue shadows are flung mindlessly from the tops of the towers;
it is quite still, just before take-off.

Seen at close range, the balloon is huge, like a many-colored
pumpkin, it shines and grows.
And the hum of the onlookers, a swarm of bumblebees;

they shout and wave to the travelers in the basket,
who pretend not to see them and keep mum about their goal.
They are immobile, and ready for the trip.

The man in the top hat still reconnoiters,
and he lifts a shiny brass tube
as if to look for clouds or something invisible.

When they rise they will be diminished to a point
till in the highest atmospheric regions they reach snow,
the whitest snow that cools and blinds

will fill the air they breathe, touch their foreheads.
In the autumn you can see it fall like frost,
the breath on high creeping over the fields,

and some autumn when the frost comes early,
you will suddenly remember them and their flight,
and how they move ever upward, in giddiness higher

through a thinner air than that of winter
with a tone like that of shattered glass
in deep forests of the most delicate rain

and how they climb ever higher through the years
until the very memory of them sings faintly like glass—
and it is intolerable; forget me, it says, believe this other.

A pleasure trip, a venture for cognoscenti.
A gentleman in a light tailcoat and bright blue vest
with a gloved hand slowly gives the signal to depart.

The balloon breaks free and already starts to rise
and the cheering imperceptibly subsides.

LARS GUSTAFSSON

Etude: The King of Denmark

It says:
The King of Denmark's cough-drops.

It says:
The *unhappy* King of Denmark's
cough-drops.

Deeply melancholy, the unhappy King
of Denmark, Holstein and his other duchies,

gazes toward us, and his large clear-blue eyes,
above his beard, over great stars and the chain,

gaze mute and inscrutible into the world
that the power loom and the steam engine

hastily change. He thinks:
I carry my fate with me,

my mysterious, unfortunate, majestic
fate. The gold pendulum strikes eleven;

muffled coughs from his aide in the antechamber's
circle of light. The King turns around at once

but sees no one.

Still wrapped in his royally deep,
unhappy sleep, the King dreams

that something remains to be explained,
something trivial and incomprehensible

something embarrassing that has to do with cough-drops.

He thinks: *We are seen by no one.*
and sinks into a deeper sleep.

Sörby Elegy

Wild chervil and chamomile surge against the base
of cinder block from the foundries that were once here.

The swallows weave an invisible web, and in here,
in softer light with the fragrance of aging wood,

here summer becomes still. Mild and patient,
as if only with great effort they remember their places

here dangle and stand things from vanishing years.
A fish net, the hoop of silvery juniper wood, that has not

held a pike since the end of World War I.
A trolling spoon constructed by Mason Ramberg,

a quiet man, who had one thumb missing.
A little boat once owned by a child

held together by very rough blocks.
A peeling garden table that was owned

by a grandmother, who lived to be one hundred.
And the shadow beneath her raspberry bushes

for a moment passes by, like a cloud,
a very tiny cloud in some other sky.

Grandfather's hammer with the shiny handle.
A mighty pair of scissors from a sheet-metal shop at Nibble.

I am presumably the last person who will remember
from where it came, from Plater Claeson at Nibble,

and after me it will be free, as free as an arrowhead
that someone finds in a riverbed among the gravel.

We give them back, but only hesitatingly and in a miserly way.
How absent-minded and mild things become,

when they are finally let loose again,
and have their long vacation, from the domain

of the human, from designs and actions and words.
How will they remember their places on tables and in drawers?

Amid the humming of wasps and the fragrance of tar, in the dark
of the small store dangle, stand and lie so many deserted things

from other years. And the June wind sweeps by.

Elisabeth Rynell
(1954–   )

Elisabeth Rynell was born in Stockholm and grew up in its suburbs. Her father was Alarik Rynell, a professor of English at the University of Stockholm; her mother was a nurse. After nine years of grade school and high school, Rynell went to London, where she worked for a year as an *au pair* girl with an English family. She then returned to complete high school and traveled afterwards to India, going by land through Iran, Afghanistan, and Pakistan. On her return home, she wrote her first book of poetry, *Lyrsvit om Gnöl*, Lyrical Suite on Grumbling, 1975). It received favorable attention in most Swedish papers, and was called cheeky, indignant, bold, and rich in metaphor.

During these years she worked at different hospitals in Stockholm and spent much time with her mother, who was stricken with cancer and died in 1975. At the same time Rynell worked on a novel.

From childhood on, Elisabeth Rynell had cherished a longing for northern Sweden, for the land of the big forests, mountains, and the wilderness. In 1977 she found a cottage almost a thousand kilometers north of Stockholm in a small village, where some ten people lived, in a pocket, as it were, outside of time and modern society. During the following years she divided her time between Stockholm and this isolated village. Her encounter with the vast forests and reindeer-herding Saami, with ancient dialects in the villages of the first settlers, and with the regal and harsh winter in these areas, became decisive in her writing, she has said in an interview. "In fact, this was for me a kind of university." Together with her husband and a new-born son, she left Stockholm for good in 1980 for a life in southern Lapland, where the family had found a small farm.

During the 1980s, Rynell published two volumes of poetry, *Sorgvingesång* (Mourningwing song, 1985) and *Sjuk fågel* (Sick bird, 1988), strongly colored by her Lapland experience. She received several prizes, including the prestigious Dan Andersson Prize, and one from the Academy of the Nine. Her husband died unexpectedly in 1987, and she was forced to leave the farm. With her two children, she moved closer to Stockholm to Norrberg, Delsbo, in the province of Hälsingland, where she now resides.

In 1990 she published her novel *En berättelse om Loka* (A story about Loka) and received stipends and prizes from several sources, among them the Swedish Academy and the Swedish PEN Club. Her novel is "told in clear, precise prose that brings the surrealist and nightmarish aspects of the narrative into relief. Elisabeth Rynell is a powerful story-teller," Rochelle Wright wrote in *World Literature Today*.

Her volume of poetry *Nattliga samtal* (Nightly conversations, 1990) is a dirge dedicated to the memory of her husband. The book was well received. "Rynell's poetry has always had the stamp of intensity and a strength which makes one associate it with that of Södergran. But in her poetry there has also been a bitter ruggedness, something ingratiating in her exact language, which also has suggested, with her sparing words, the tone of popular ballads," Eva Ström wrote in *Sydsv. Dagbladet*.

In addition to her work in fiction, Rynell writes articles and essays on various political and ideological questions. She also teaches courses in creative writing, has traveled around the country, and written poetry for children. She is a member of the board of belles lettres in the Association of Swedish Authors and has been active in several other authors' organizations.

The youngest poet in this volume, she writes this self-characterization in *Sjuk fågel*:

> Time is a
> knife
> which cuts me loose from
> myself
> I
> am a
> stranger here
> with an incomprehensible dialect from
> some distant parish.

The poem "Body Language" (included here) was written during one night in Stockholm. "I remember that I wrote it so to speak, polemically, against thoughts expressed by a young Danish poet, Søren Ulric Thomsen. The poem was originally entitled 'Poetics' in protest against a narrow-minded view of the body, of humanity, and of poetry."

"This-That" was conceived and written while she lived in a small house in southern Lapland. There was a terrific storm and she was filled with a feeling that something in this wild storm out there in the night, as it were, knocked at a door, inside her, as if the storm wanted to deliver a message. "And a strong feeling of presence, my presence, and the presence of 'cosmos' in a big tangle pervaded me," she wrote in a letter.

Body Language

They say
that I must lay myself
and you too little child
and you my beloved
and the Father and the Mother
and the Aunt and the great Cloud Spirit
roughly
and finely cut
indiscriminately
on the big Assembly Line
Foot Elbow joint Nails Trunk
all your Hair one by one
    Tongue Sex thin Lips
grip
by grip
to be pulled to pieces
                    But
it is not my Mouth
kissing you Beloved
               It is
my unreasonable love
crying kisses through my mouth
And my tongue's play in your mouth
is your sex growing in me,
the very river
that rises and rises
above the boats and the boat-houses

~

indeed are we not fish
twirling around one another
                              And the sea also
with our continual clasping
in wave after wave?

Listen! My breath
pervades all trees
and filters between the leaves
                              My body
is the very suspension
of my body
My hand
touches you so that you become part of me—
grazes your skin
and is dissolved
                              I
am not divisible
I am the root of minus one
My shoulder
is a finger

My hand
is a foot
        My sex
        an eye
although it resembles
a vessel on the open sea
                        And I know
that if I embrace the birch tree long enough
it will enclose me in its hard flesh

and eat me with a tree's
thorough slowness
                        Look! I am a birch tree
and the sap rises to my head
and all my innumerable leaves
twitter deafeningly in my network of branches
My roots
              reach down into the sea
where the fish play hide-and-seek in my convolutions
and forests of algae sway beneath them
like dreams
When I speak
                    I am silent.
                              Give me
your hand.

It is a river
that obliterates shores.
And the words go
upstream through the rapids
                              Seeking
tranquillity
where sky sinks into water
bathing its clouds and birds
and washes itself clean
of dust.

This-That

It scratches on the door
I open It
comes in
and fills me

That the stars are so many,
And the wind precisely as strong
as here in my deepest
autumn darkness.
My little house
stands and trembles
on the wind's forefinger
The trees dance and howl
round about
ever wilder
They wish something of me
the stars
in their geometric meaninglessness
they expose me
to a more immense emptiness
a fulfillment without a goal
the impossible
in myriads
of stars

That the trees stand and sway there
sway and are transformed
and become a people
eternal wanderers

who pitch their camp and become forests
and move on
with raised flutes at the farthest point
between their fingers
as if constantly vibrating
with fearless song
and then play rain with birds
and shake water out of themselves like laughter
and look on when stars reign
over empty spaces and houses
that have come loose
while patiently in ring after ring
they assemble to dance
and stamping and howling
filter wind between themselves
and move between empty spaces
hither and thither
according to a lawlessness
that reigns firmly

THERE IS A SCRATCHING AT THE DOOR

I OPEN   IT

COMES IN

AND FILLS ME

That I. And stand here.
The throng up there
in my chest
Transformations
       and entire peoples
That I.

In all the interspaces
Wash through me
Hither and thither
As between light and darkness
A house vibrating
on a fingertip
And stand here
Turning slowly
to stamping surging
invisible music   That
I
and really
really so many stars
blowing in the black firmament
Then silence
and trees that slowly awaken
and break up from their night encampments
clouded
mumbling
again start
moving

No it has no beginning and
no end
Where the wind
picks up its wind
its message with indecipherable script
And through one's marrow and through valleys
this That
mostly like a flute
or a presentiment of something
rocked in the wind's cradle

The Vanishing

You wish to pull yourself together
for a leap
right into the world
inside
the world.
You wish to enter the room Absence
and fill it. You rave about
entering the tree
and being its branches' full expression.
You beat your face
until it bursts asunder
You know
that behind the silken paper of your skin
there is a sky that is more real. And
when you kiss your beloved
your mouth never comes
sufficiently close
and your tongue
nearly breaks loose from its root
in order to help you out
of your loneliness.

Sick Bird

If I could speak.
If I could wind myself up into song
If I could have the words borne out through a flute.
The birds appear sick. The traffic circles stare
hollow-eyed into their center. And no
word. No brazen blustery
word. The permafrost wedges itself
ever deeper into the earth. The clocks
tick. Who is it
who pounds inside
me? No,
there are no nice children here. But only snow.
Still it is a consolation that no one meant anything
in particular by the snow. Not by me either.
And there is a wind up in the mountains.
A strong wind.
A good wind that will put everything right.
A good wind that will put everything right.

Before the Words

It was simple then.
It was before there were words
I was a boundless room

There I was yellow grass
There were faces of brick
There ditches crossed each other
on an endless plain

It was simple then.
I lived in animal eyes
Large, seeing
People swarming with
faces

The days devoured one another
and grew into one another
The yellow sunlight leapt
in a thick cylinder
from the loudspeaker
Inside the cylinder
millions of dust particles danced
as if they were music

On certain days there was wind and sharp light
On others there were shadows
and incomprehensible curtains

in narrow gray rooms
The words were songs
a game of the mouth and the tongue
a gurgling
on jubilant feet

It was simple then.
It was before there were words
There were no roads
Milk filled my mouth
and there was constant transformation

The Absence of a House

I see wild-grown grass on a color photograph.
A little blurred. A faint trace
of a hill. Young raspberry thickets
and tall violet flowers.
Some trees round about.
Pines.

And I suddenly recognize them
as a pattern inside myself.
As a tangle of ever more distant roads
or root fibers
deeper down
in the compressed blackness.

How gently the trunks bent down
How the branches crept out of them
How the bark shone
through the dark from an inner orange

Here a plot of land arose
from the raspberry thicket
Dinners on flowery porcelain
the clatter of an iron gate
a harbor and mounds of sulfur
where a little girl walks between the legs
of huge crane operators

~

And old castle
with a dungeon,
a black-lacquered mine
exhibited on a hill
and a war by the sea where the secret
little trains
rolled in concrete bunker tunnels

A pier
led out into the sea,
a girl with sand between the lips of her sex
in tin cans collected grasshoppers with broken legs

A country
with a house in the middle
that contained all the rooms of my dreams
and secret rooms
                            arose from the raspberry thicket
I recognized it
in the trees
in their bowing to one another
their finest gesture
and in the absence
of a house.

Four Reductions

I.

This, one cannot depict. It is too shiny, has no secrets; one's glance rebounds from it. No shadow draws out the invisible. Huge mountain ridges in the darkness. One can't see it. Time is like a drawn-out piercing scream, sirens from a thousand invisible ambulances. I am afraid. Everybody seems so kind. Smile. Look away. No one here speaks in a loud voice or gesticulates wildly. Everyone is on his way on some important errand. Everyone makes allowances for me. For everything. For anything at all.

Conversing, we are carried past one another in a perfect dance. Without even brushing against one another. I try to muster my courage. I start over every morning. Try to engender hope, where it flings itself between the treetops. To hold onto something I think. Hard and relentlessly. (The little fledgling: the world, hot, ticking. Surging greenery. A moment only—yes, indeed, a little parenthesis of light, gingerly wedged in between the dark. And the thin body becomes a feather heavier in my hand, the head falls slowly backward—; lifeless feather ball, you had a feverish dream: the field's merciless greenery, rustling masses of leaves, the sun's burning eye. All this. Then—gone.)

I send down my downy root fibers ever deeper into the earth. Hunting for a stronghold down there in the blindness, a little nest. They grope about like ivy. Creeping arms. Suction feet. Winding-whorling. I want to cling onto it here. I want to prove that life is possible; put in the shadows that bring out your face. Now that the great lack of faith is being preached to us. And the last sacrament is being prepared in the laboratories. The procrustean terror of reduction. I believe. I believe in a life after this one.

Five Stills

Our first night together. Remember how I padded across the floor and snuggled into bed with you. How our hands. And mouths. Just so, I thought. That mouth I had waited for. We trembled inside touching each other almost chastely. We could not sleep. We were so awake. So startled.

Perhaps at dawn we slept for a while.

The next morning strangely hung over, we drove through Sörmland. It was a mild quiet November day. We stopped by an old mill. The millhouse as such was gone, but its foundation was still there. And the smooth, reflecting pond. We crawled into the mill-wheel through a hole in the stone wall. Sat silently crouched in there and experienced the power, the thumping, the deadly peril if the huge wheel had been in motion.

It was curiously quiet. We experienced something else as well. You and I suddenly were set in place as in a piece of jewelry. Our lives. And such a silence settling over our encounter.

*

I have seen on a photograph how my eyes looked afterwards. Shining. Almost insane. In the next picture you sit with our son in your arms. Then they moved the bed out into the corridor. There I lay with the child next to me. And my handbag and my clothes at the foot of the bed. You were sitting on the edge of the bed. We were in the light. It was like a painting done long ago. We were the only ones in it. No one could reach into it and no one could take it away from us. I saw it from another angle in the room, as if we were an inner image, a depiction of something in a dream.

But just before, my body trembled, when they put the child on my stomach. And I raised my hands incredibly slowly and held them protectively around it.

*

Certain nights were like fireworks of screams with the hatred drumming and kicking against the walls of the house. One Easter night I fled from the house, out into the snow beneath an austere and ice-cold sky. I climbed up into the barn and dug down in the hay and heard the wind howl in all the crevices of the wall. With rage within me like a fire-storm, I was warm and awake.

Finally you found me. You asked me to come. But I remained in the hay which pricked me on the back of my neck. And I swore a solemn oath always firmly to hate you as I do now.

Then strange sounds were heard from the lower part of the barn. There a ewe stood bellowing in labor. I rushed through the dawn and fetched you. Together we saw two white lambs being forced out into the raw-cold world. And we stood close together. And it was very beautiful.

*

I sat on the sofa. I was wearing a large black skirt. A skirt that was almost like a living entity. Heavy, wide and rustling. You came up to me. You smiled a little and looked at me all the time, while gingerly you pulled off what there was of panties underneath the skirt.

Then there was only my bare body there under the cloth. Like a small, wild, spirited animal. My bottom, my thighs, my lap—and then your hands.

We played all evening. And the great black skirt kept your face hidden. And the great black darkness out there. And the children asleep up there. You took off my sweater and drank my breasts in deep gulps. I peeled you down white and clear. Finally there was only the rustling skirt. It was night. We took that off also. We were more naked than ever. Nothing but skin. Down on the floor.

*

We had a dream together. A landscape. Very quiet. The ptarmigans invisible in the snow. C. F. Hill had painted the fir trees there. And the mountains in their silence. Naked sunrise and sunset. Let the winds wreak havoc. It was tremendous, although quiet. Like a Buddha I saw once. There were a few houses but mainly one saw the streams of smoke rising into the sky. There the clouds sailed like boats, right above our faces. Summer was heavenly, red-hot. Then white alpine flowers grew. Cloud shadows crossed between the mountains. And we stood there hand in hand, seized by a longing that proved to be greater than ourselves. The agitated waters of Great Lake Ara. The land that stretched out quietly in all directions. Our house on the hill, so close to the sky. It was a prayer that we uttered together, almost frightened by our gravity.

About the Editor

William Jay Smith has been a prolific writer, publishing over fifty books of poetry, literary criticism, children's poetry, translations, and memoirs, in addition to editing several anthologies. Two of his ten books of poetry were final contenders for the National Book Award, and his children's poems appear regularly in anthologies throughout the English-speaking world. Smith has translated poetry from several languages, and for his translations has received medals from the French Academy and the Hungarian government. With Leif Sjöberg, he translated from the Swedish *Agadir* by Artur Lundkvist and *Wild Bouquet: Nature Poems* by Harry Martinson. He was Consultant in Poetry to the Library of Congress (a post now called Poet Laureate) 1968–1970, and has taught at Williams College, Columbia University, and Hollins College, of which he is Professor Emeritus. Among his books are *Collected Poems 1939–1989* (Scribner's), *Army Brat: A Memoir* (Story Line Press), *Laughing Time: Collected Nonsense* (Farrar, Straus & Giroux), and *Birds and Beasts* (David Godine).

About the Translator

Leif Sjöberg, Professor Emeritus, Scandinavian Studies and Comparative Literature at Stony Brook, New York, has collaborated with W. H. Auden (Hammarskjöld, *Markings* and Ekelöf, *Selected Poems*); Muriel Rukeyser (Ekelöf, *A Mölna Elegy*); May Swenson (Tranströmer, *Windows & Stones*); William Jay Smith (Martinson, *Wild Bouquet* and Lundkvist, *Agadir*). With Professor Stephen Klass he translated Martinson's *Aniara, a review of man in space and time,* and Sara Lidman's *Cranewater Chronicles*.